ARE YOU KIDDING ME?

MY LIFE WITH AN EXTREMELY LOUD FAMILY, BATHROOM CALAMITIES, AND CRAZY RELATIVES

STACEY GUSTAFSON

LUMINARE PRESS

EUGENE, OREGON

The following stories were previously published in the Pleasanton Patch: No Santa, No Way; My Family Is Loud; Fashion Fail; School's Out for the Summer; Extremely Loud and Incredibly Close; What Women Really Want; The Rewrapper; Tea Party; War in the Skies; Going Commando; Hair Gone Wild; Toilet Phobia; I'm Going Straight to Hell; More Napkins Please; Fancy Meeting You Here; I Survived the Playground; For Your Eyes Only

Are You Kidding Me? My Life With an Extremely Loud Family, Bathroom Calamities, and Crazy Relatives
© 2014 Stacey Gustafson

Printed in the United States of America

Cover Design: Claire Last

Luminare Press
467 W 17th Ave
Eugene, OR 97401
www.luminarepress.com

LCCN: 2014946642

ISBN: 978-1-937303-31-0

To Mike, Ashley and Brock.
whose sense of humor is unmatched.

The family. We were a strange little band of characters trudging through life sharing diseases and toothpaste, coveting one another's desserts, hiding shampoo, borrowing money, locking each other out of our rooms, inflicting pain and kissing to heal it in the same instant, loving, laughing, defending, and trying to figure out the common thread that bound us all together.
—Erma Bombeck

CONTENTS

UNLESS YOU'RE BLEEDING OR ON FIRE, DON'T CALL ME!

THINK LIKE A MAN, BUT DON'T THINK TOO LONG

WHEN LIFE GIVES YOU LEMONS, THROW THEM BACK HARD

IT'S ALL RELATIVE
UNTIL THEY DRIVE ME CRAZY

HELLO, MY NAME IS STACEY...

Have you ever faked a heart attack in church to avoid shaking hands during the sign of peace? Are your teen-agers embarrassed by your driving, your clothing, and your fear of public restrooms? Climb aboard *Are You Kidding Me?* as I tackle my fear of aging, my family's shaky grasp of sharing and my wonder over the fact that I'm married to a man who kills the lawn but expects "favors" for conquering a steak on the barbeque.

My story isn't much different than yours. Classic girl meets boy. Gets married. Moves to the suburbs. Buys a house. Girl quits job. A new baby girl. A new baby boy. Kids grow up and start to leave the nest. Girl hopes there is more to life than dirty laundry, carpool, and being a sex slave. Got your attention?

Let me start at the beginning. I always loved to read. Each summer I borrowed one hundred books from the public library. I couldn't get enough of Nancy Drew or *Little House on the Prairie*. I escaped into a world of mysteries, adventures and dreamed of places to visit one day.

Around eighth grade my parents got divorced. I knew they both loved me, but they had married too young and couldn't make it work. During that time, my mom was very sad. That's when I discovered the power of comedy. I could make her laugh her butt off. I imitated Mick Jagger and Elvis, or the guy next door. Or my father. I could spin a funny rap song like nobody's business. And for a little bit she would laugh instead of cry. That gave me power.

In high school, I wanted to be the next great journalist, like Barbara Walters. I was Editor in Chief of the school newspaper, the *Troubadour,* and received the outstanding student award for English at graduation. When I entered college, I picked math as my major. Go figure.

I married my college sweetheart and we've been together for twenty-five years. He changed my life. He makes me laugh so hard I pee in my pants a little bit. Our kids have a great sense of humor too. Comedy is our family's Krazy Glue. We don't take ourselves too seriously. We've lived in seven states from the east to the west coast. You could say we get around.

As the kids started to grow up and out, I noticed something was missing and I filled the void with writing. Not to be overly dramatic, but it kept me sane. I bundled up all my frustrations and oozed them out onto paper, one pain-in-the-ass problem at a time and it felt good.

When I share my work, people laugh and can relate. That's because my problems are like yours. Does your husband need to be reminded each week to take out the trash? So does mine. Do your kids complain about everything from the way you drive to your fashion sense? Mine too. Do the holidays cause you to overdose on Maalox? See what I mean? You're just like me except I write about it, much to the chagrin of my family.

Grab a coffee, relax and have a good laugh on my behalf. I don't mind.

UNLESS YOU'RE BLEEDING OR ON FIRE, DON'T CALL ME!

A TRAINING OPPORTUNITY

"Let's go. Are you ready? Why are we still standing here? Do you think I have all day?" my daughter nags. Burning rubber like a NASCAR contender, we zoom to the nearest department store.

At the mall, we shop for the many back-to-school needs of a nine-year-old girl: school supplies, school shirts, jazzy headbands, cool jeans and…bras. In keeping with my promise, my daughter and I search for bras. Underwire, padded, strapless, backless—the styles of bras are endless. But today, we shop to satisfy my daughter's desire to be a mature young lady. We seek a training bra.

She enters the lingerie department in a trance. Different colors and varieties of bras hang across the junior department, like a sea of flags at the United Nations. My daughter looks around in wonder, preparing to enter preadolescence one bra at a time.

After much contemplation, we complete our selections. White and simple, these are bras a mother dreams about for her daughter. With purchases in hand, we march to the only checkout lane open and drop the items on the counter.

Dark-haired and attractive, our teenage clerk, Kyle, turns to face us. With a flash of pearly whites he asks, "Did you find everything you need?"

My daughter and I smile knowingly at each other, our purchases forming a bond between us that only a mother and daughter can experience. She is growing up.

Kyle scans our purchases and I hear only one soft beep. But, how can that be? We selected two bras. My mind wrestles with the pros and cons of the next step. Two choices exist: we slip out of the store quietly, stealing the bra that didn't scan, or I humiliate my daughter and possibly the store clerk by pointing out his error. I decide to be honest. After all, I am a parent—a role model.

"Wait! You only rang up one bra. You missed the other one."

By my side, my daughter melts like butter on a hot plate. Kyle attempts to pull apart the AAA training bras tangled together. I reach over to help, and the tug of war begins. As he yanks upward, I jerk to the left and right.

"Thanks a lot. This is the most humiliating day of my life," whispers my daughter. Kyle avoids eye contact and my daughter tries to hide behind my purse. I quickly glide my Visa card across the scanner to pay. Then we charge through the automated doors and out of the store. Ashley stays close by my side, still grumbling and embarrassed.

"Mom, he was the cutest boy! And did you notice how embarrassed he was?"

Bra shopping is not for the meek. Maybe my husband was right to stay home, avoiding the whole thing. Despite the checkout debacle, my daughter lights up in anticipation of trying on each training bra. Once home, she puts on the bras over her tank top and prances around the room, modeling her updated figure for her dad and brother. My son yells at her to quit blocking the TV, but Dad offers her the attention she craves.

"Yes, Ashley, you look all grown up."

Smiling and glowing, she confidently strolls out of the room.

CLASS CLOWN

Parent-teacher conferences are as unsettling as being attacked on a city street by a flock of geese overdosed on Ex-Lax. You hope you don't get hit with something you weren't expecting.

When our son brought home a crumpled-up reminder note about his upcoming parent-teacher conference, my husband said to me, "Should we be concerned?"

"Nah," I said with a laugh. "We've got nothing to fear. Our little guy's fun-loving, smart, and inquisitive. He's right on track."

I was certain his bubbly kindergarten teacher would load on the compliments with a flash of her professionally whitened teeth and say, "Your son is fabulous. A model student."

This would be a piece of cake.

I prepared a list of questions for Ms. Smiley, things like, "Is our child working to the best of his ability? Is he a visual, auditory or tactile learner?"

The day of the conference we peeked at the parent-teacher appointment list taped on the classroom door and confirmed it was the correct room at the right time.

My husband and I entered the classroom with a grin and took a seat at our boy's tiny desk. The perky young teacher beamed down at us from her stool, hands folded in her lap.

Let the bragging begin.

With a serious face, she said, "I love your son's energy. He is certainly enthusiastic, but ...."

No buts. What do you mean, but?

She continued, "But yard-duty volunteers are concerned he's causing a commotion at recess. Personally, I embrace his enthusiasm."

Whew!

"What's he doing?"

"He has single-handedly taught the whole kindergarten class how to armpit fart. No worries. I think boys should be boys," she said with a giggle.

At the doorway, a woman with a deep voice cleared her throat and said, "When you're finished here, do you mind dropping by the gymnasium?" and scooted off with a flash of spiky, black hair.

"Who's that?" I asked his teacher.

"Your son's physical education instructor, Ms. Wagner. Not sure what she wants," she said with a twist of her ponytail. "As I was saying, he's a pleasure to have in class. Mom and Dad, you're doing a good job."

You bet we are!

I winked at my husband and gripped his hand as we strutted down the hallway to the gym. Ms. Wagner straightened the exercise mats and flagged us over to her corner office.

"Thanks for coming by," she said, running a hand through her hair. "I want to start out by saying that I enjoy having your son in class but I'm concerned about his safety and the well-being of the other kids."

Woman, what are you talking about?

"He's the biggest boy in class, and I'm afraid he's going to hurt the other children."

"What's he doing?" I said with a frown.

"Let me give you an example. Right now the class is doing gymnastics, practicing log rolls and somersaults on the mats. Yesterday, he rolled across his mat, knocked down the other children, then rolled over their bodies and out the gymnasium door," she said rubbing the back of her neck. "We're just concerned about his safety."

Oh my God! Like a human army tank!

"I don't want to take up any more of your time," she said, pushing back her chair and standing up. "Please try to get your kid under control."

With a weak handshake, we left the gym, our heads held in shame. As we rushed down the hallway to get the hell out of there, a tall, bearded man with fashionable glasses blocked our way. "Glad I bumped into you," he said, looking us up and down. "I'm Mr. Thompson, your son's music teacher. Can you stop by for thirty seconds?"

"Uh…sure," we said in unison.

Oh boy, our son is a musical prodigy!

Once in the music room, we plopped down on the metal risers next to the teacher.

"First, I want to tell you that your child has a very high level of energy."

"Okay," I said, sneaking a look at my husband.

"He's disrupting the class," he blurted out.

"Can you give us an example?"

"Let me show you," he said as he hoisted himself up in true dramatic fashion. We stared, eyes wide and mouths open, as a six-foot three-inch giant hopped around the classroom like a one-legged kangaroo and slapped his butt with wooden drumsticks.

We departed the room holding onto each other, unable to suppress the laughter any longer. I glanced over my shoulder and spied the teacher as he chuckled too and dabbed his eyes with a tissue.

Geez, our son, the five-year-old class clown. Like I said, you never know what will hit you at the parent-teacher conference.

GOOD PETS GONE BAD

When my kids were younger, they begged for a hamster. For Easter we surprised them with a brown, long-haired teddy bear hamster, the perfect gateway pet. We purchased all the essentials: a modular hamster habitat complete with tree house, tunnels and a wheel ($40.89); an exercise ball ($23.98); and chew toys ($3.99).

Our kids (sort of) played with Chubby Cheeks for about three months and then ignored him. Then the hamster grew a tumor. Not just any tumor, but one that oozed; a pus-filled, weeping, disgustingly red tumor.

Soon the hamster was living in the laundry room. Since I washed all the clothes, it became my task to feed and care for him. But after another month "the hamster problem" needed to be addressed.

"Hey, kids, come into the living room," I said, staring down at my hands. "The hamster needs to go to PetSmart. His tumor needs to be examined."

"We still have a hamster?" said my son.

Whose kid is this?

The next morning, I placed Chubby Cheeks in a box and drove to the vet. After the doctor examined him, we met in the waiting room. He said, "Good news. We can operate and remove the tumor. What would you like us to do?"

"Hmmm…how much will it cost?"

"$300," he said, checking his watch.

"Do you mind if I ask my husband first?"

I called my hubby and explained the problem. He listened without interruption for a few minutes. After a long pause I asked, "So what should we do? Operate? They can squeeze it in today."

"How much does a new hamster cost?" he asked.

"Five dollars."

Problem solved.

NO SANTA, NO WAY

Details were sketchy, but within moments, on Christmas Day, Santa was history, and our daughter was ticked.

That evening, unwrapped packages and children's toys were scattered throughout the living room and the memory of Christmas was starting to fade. I cleaned up the silver tinsel and crumpled wrapping paper, and Dad offered to tuck the kids into bed.

"Goodnight little ones," I said with big hugs and kisses. "Santa was very good to you this year."

Off to bed they crawled. But suddenly, from across the house, an earsplitting cry, a sob, and a tear? Our daughter came running back into the room, pointing wildly at the magazine she was holding. "This can't be true! I just found out there is no Santa. It says right here," she cried. Time to come clean. We had planned to stretch out jolly Ol' St. Nick until our youngest was in second grade. We knew once the truth was out, it would only be a matter of time before our daughter would spill the beans to her younger brother. If he pushed her buttons the wrong way, the tale would roll off her tongue like syrup on pancakes. She'd drop the bomb: "There is no Santa Claus."

We pleaded with her to keep the secret for a bit longer and for her troubles, we left an extra gift under the tree the next Christmas. She joined the big kids on the block and discovered that there was more to Christmas than a Game Boy, DVDs and a new bike. She looked deeply into our eyes and declared, "I will keep Santa alive in my heart!"

Days later, crisis averted, we visited Grandma in the Midwest. She anticipated sharing the secret with an adult, someone in the know, just like herself.

On the plane ride, she started to wiggle a loose tooth. She turned to me with a shocked expression and said, "Do you mean there isn't a Tooth Fairy either?"

"Nope, that's me," I said with a giggle.

"And the Easter Bunny?" she asked in a shaky voice.

"Me again."

"Waaa!!!!!!!!"

FLYING FINGERNAIL FIASCO

I've spent a lot of time saying "no" to my daughter's requests.

"Can I eat a brownie sundae for breakfast?"

"Nope," I said.

"Can I ride my bike twenty miles across town?"

"Negative."

"Can I skip school this week?"

"Nada."

"You should lighten up," my husband said. "Let Ashley try new things and see how it goes." *He's not only good-looking, he's smart!*

I noticed my feisty fifth-grader taking an interest, for the first time, in boys, lipstick and bras. Just last week, she asked to borrow my beauty supplies.

"Can I use your mascara?" she said, holding her breath.

"No, you're too young." I laughed.

"How 'bout concealer?"

"Nope, your skin's beautiful. You don't need it."

Whether I liked it or not, I couldn't stop her from growing up. I would eventually have to let her test new stuff on her own.

"Mom, some girls are wearing fake fingernails in my class," she said over dinner. "Can I try?"

At last, my chance to turn no into yes.

"Sure, let's go shopping and you can pick out a set," I said with a wink to her father.

"Yippee!" she said, twirling her blond ponytail and skipping away.

At Target, she zoomed to the beauty-supply aisle. Racks of brilliant eye shadow, glossy lip gel, glittery nail polish, and cosmetic brushes beckoned.

"These are the ones," she said, lips parting. She pointed her raggedy nails at "Glamor Girl Ultra-Long Adhesive Nails." With a pre-adhesive backing, one pressed down for five seconds and *ta-da*. These were stiletto nails reserved for experts.

"Are you sure you want the longest ones?" I asked. "Maybe something shorter would be better for your first try."

"Nope, these are the ones," she said, with a gleam in her eye.

"Okey-dokey."

Once home, she systematically fanned ten fancy fake fingernails on the kitchen table. With the precision of a plastic surgeon, she adhered each with tweezers. Next, she lavished on electric pink polish and waited for them to dry.

Dad ambled into the room and flagged me over. "What's going on?" he whispered. "You let her buy those?"

Ashley caught his eye, wiggled her fingers in front of his face and said, "Dad, take a look."

He grabbed his cheeks in disbelief, took a step back and said, "Wow! Wow!"

For Ashley, this was the highest compliment. She hugged Dad around the waist and rushed out of the house to show off her manicure to the kid next door.

Problems kicked off that evening. She hollered, "Mom, can you come in and help me?"

Difficulties? Shocking!

"What's wrong?"

"I can't pull up my pajama bottoms. These dang nails are getting in the way."

Surprise. My plan is gelling nicely.

"No problem," I said with a sigh. "But by school tomorrow you'll need to figure out a way to do it yourself."

Before bedtime she begged for help again to take out her contacts, brush her teeth and operate the remote control.

This was getting good.

Next morning, I yelled goodbye from the front porch as she hopped on the bus. She waved out the window like a pageant queen aboard a parade float.

After school I asked, "How was the first day with your new nails?"

"Awesome. All the girls thought they were so pretty. Only one fell off."

I held her hand and stared at the errant nail, reattached haphazardly. *By the end of the week, she'll look like Edward Scissorhands!*

Day two:

"I pulled off two nails on my right hand so I could finish my homework. Being beautiful is a lot of work," she said, glancing down at her fingers.

Day three:

"How'd it go today?" I said as I stared in amazement

at her nails, mangled or missing.

"I think I better take these dumb things off. A few flew off in class and kids had to help me find them. I lost three."

"By the way, you have a nail stuck in your ponytail," I said, offering Dad a thumbs-up behind her back.

Mission accomplished.

MY FAMILY IS LOUD

Like fans at a Brazilian soccer match, my family is loud. I crave moments of silence, seeking times I can avoid the thunder, everyone talking at once, doors slamming, television blaring, kids fighting, general noise pollution.

Saturday morning, I peek at the clock; it's 8:30 a.m. My daughter and son are sound asleep. Tiptoeing down the stairs, I start my morning ritual: I prepare coffee, grab a novel and plop on the sofa. All mine. A few blissful moments of silence. I crack open my book and begin to read the first page.

But wait. I tilt my head towards the staircase. *You've got to be kidding.* My husband should be sound asleep; he just returned from a week in Japan. And I am certain the kids will stay in bed until 11 a.m. since there are no activities scheduled for this weekend.

But there it is: clomp, clomp, clomp. My husband descends, quiet as a Clydesdale. He mumbles a weary "Good morning" and reaches for the object of his affection, the Cuisinart Brew Central 1200 Coffee Maker.

He shoves aside other appliances. Rattle, rattle, thunder, clatter, boom. Then he removes the coffee grinder from the cabinet, dumps in a cup of beans, pushes the top, and whirls away. Like a buzz saw, the racket shatters the silence. After fifteen seconds, he pushes the top down again for good measure. I cringe as he turns coffee beans into powder.

Clearing his throat, he says, "Want some?"

"No thanks. I'm fine." *Why are you so noisy!*

He grabs the weekend paper, snapping the pages each time he finishes a section. Snap, crinkle, crinkle, hmmmmm. On it goes, page by torturous page, snap, crinkle, crinkle. He sighs to himself and attempts to engage me in conversation about one sports story after another. *Trying to relax here, mister.*

Still on page one of my novel, *Why My Third Husband Will Be a Dog*.

Thirty minutes later, like a herd of rhinos, my son and daughter stomp down the staircase in search of food. A fight erupts over cereal.

"Where's the good cereal? What happened to the O's?" my son asks.

Oh please, not the Honey Graham O's. On a noise-o-meter, it registers at 100 decibels—not recommended without earplugs.

He pours a big bowl, fakes to the left, kicks the empty box into the trashcan and starts to munch. And crunch and crunch and slurp and smack.

My daughter whines, "You ate all the good cereal. The rest is gross."

She rummages around the pantry, pooh-poohing one box after another. Metal pots and pans bounce off the shelf and drop onto the tile floor. Crash, whiz, bang. I cannot stop my hands from shaking.

After forty-five minutes, I am only on page ten. Can't remember a thing. Must reread. Again.

Briiiiiing.

"Mom, phone," screams my son as he hands me the phone.

Sally from All Star Sports says, "The stuff you ordered is in. Stop by anytime to get it."

"Thanks. And do you have any blue athletic socks in stock?" I ask.

"What?"

"Socks. Do you carry blue socks?"

"Can't hear you. How many kids do you have? Sounds like you're running a daycare center."

Tell me about it.

Within moments, they rush upstairs, yelling and laughing. With quivering hands, I turn back to page one. In the living room, my husband listens to *The Wall Street Journal* on the iPad, high volume. Reruns of the Warrior's game run wildly on the television in the background. Thousands of screaming, chanting fans. I imagine the house vibrating.

My eyelid starts to spasm and my head jerks to the right. He notices the tics and asks, "Are you okay? Your eye's bugging out."

"Trying to read a book. I'll go in the other room."

I've heard that too much noise can cause increased levels of anxiety, tinnitus and hearing loss. I head for shelter at the nearest safe place.

If you need me, I'll be hiding in the upstairs closet, reading.

FASHION FAIL

"Mom, it wouldn't hurt for you to dress up a little before you drop us off at school," says my thirteen-year-old daughter.

And by "a little" she means stiletto heels, coiffed hair, and full makeup. Her fashion icon is a friend's mother who has the audacity to be cool and put together by eight a.m. She wears trendy pumps, coordinated jewelry, and designer sunglasses—a true fashion aficionado. Heck, I'm lucky to swing that on a long weekend. What kind of mother wears three-inch heels to walk the kids to school?

Not to be excluded from the conversation, my ten-year-old son chimes in, "Seriously, Mom. It's embarrassing. Try to look better."

Who is he kidding? Having five inches of boxer shorts hanging over the top of his blue jeans doesn't qualify as fashion sense. His personal style includes hair Andy Warhol would envy and breath that melts wallpaper. Me embarrass him? Oy vey!

"By the way, you have permanent black marker on your face," I say.

Okay, I admit, there may be some merit to their complaints. My fashion sins are innumerable. The standard uniform in the morning consists of whatever I wore to bed the night before, usually an old baggy T-shirt and ratty sweatpants. Putting on a bra is the only concession I make prior to driving them to school. After all, I justify, I'm only visible to others from the waist up. I might put in contacts instead of wearing eyeglasses, but why push it?

But, I give a shot at improving my appearance, for the kids' sake. Getting up an hour earlier the next day, I shower, blow dry, mousse, even use the fancy imported boar-bristle brush recommended by my stylist. After flecking off a few suspicious white pieces of fur clinging to the top of my head, I realize the dog brush is strangely similar to the $49 professional hair styling brush. On the plus side, both keep tangles and mats at bay. Perfect.

In the makeover process, I surprise myself by feeling better, more confident. So I continue primping. New straight-leg jeans with a billowy top. Full makeup. Eye shadow. A spritz of perfume to round out the "new me." No time to make the kids' lunch or breakfast—too busy grooming. I reassure myself that they can assume more responsibility around the house and help with basic chores like getting their own meals. It is good for them.

Voilà! I approach the kids in the kitchen warily. The moment of impact is one to savor. As usual, it takes them awhile to notice that I'm in the room. They gasp at my transformation as I enjoy their astonishment for a few moments.

"Time to go," I say. "Grab your stuff and we'll just make it before the bell rings!"

The shock on their faces is a toss between amazement and fear. "But Mom! What about breakfast? We've been waiting. And where's the homework you were supposed to sign? You didn't bother to iron my shirt."

In response to their grumbling, I say, "Sorry guys. We've got to go to school. But what do you think about how I look? Do I make you proud?" Shrugs and confusion fill their little faces. Used to being the objects of my constant focus, they do not know how to reply.

"You look better than usual, I guess," mumbles Baggy Pants.

"Can I get some new clothes too?" asks Ms. Fashion.

Despite their attitude, I decide to proceed with the experiment a bit longer and maybe learn something about myself in the process. Dressing up makes everyone feel nice. Who am I to judge others who take hours getting decked out? As a compromise, I'll spend an extra ten minutes each morning in order to feel good about my appearance and please the kids at the same time. No more embarrassing moments in the carpool lane. No more bolting from the car, anxious to avoid having their friends witness my slovenly ways.

The next morning, my son says, "Mom, your hair looks okay today."

Now, that's a compliment if I ever heard one. My daughter even praises my clothing choice and gives me two thumbs up. And that other over-dressed mother? Who cares! Despite the urge to press on the gas pedal a teeny bit when I see her at the crosswalk, I discover that she's the inspiration I need to change my lazy style. Gotta go. I've got an appointment at Nordstrom for a full face and body makeover. Vroom! Vroom!

SCHOOL'S OUT FOR THE SUMMER

A few years ago, after dropping my kids off at middle school, I met a couple of friends at Starbucks. The conversation went something like this:

"So, what'd you get on your report card?" I asked, tapping a venti latte with my nails.

"Five A's, 2B's. How about you?" said another mom as she checked her cell phone.

"Four A's, one B and one C. Took me two parent-teacher meetings and a call to the principal to get the C," I said.

"Try harder next time."

Let me be the first to admit I help my kids way too much. From typing lengthy, boring essays at midnight to checking tedious math homework before breakfast, I can't stop helping. Heck, I've even finished their chores and done homework assignments.

But, I am adult enough to realize that I can't stop helping because it makes me feel needed. I'm part of the problem, and it's time to break the cycle. Stage One—Denial.

Here's what happened two days before the end of the school year. My son strolled into the house after hanging out with friends and announced, "I need to turn in a Kleenex box for extra credit or I'll get a B in class. School's short on supplies."

"What!? How did you let it come down to the wire?" I said, hunching my shoulders.

"I don't know," he said, walking away without so much as a backward glance.

After my daughter returned home from school, it was more of the same.

"I need a costume for my speech tomorrow," she said, twirling her hair around a pencil.

"What speech?" I asked.

"I'm playing the role of Stella for *A Streetcar Named Desire*."

"What does she wear?"

"I have no idea," she said as she sauntered down the hallway. "And I need to bring a pan of brownies to Spanish."

I made a mental list of all I would have to do tomorrow. I realized that while my kids would be signing yearbooks, cleaning out old homework, and making plans for the summer, I would be doing their dirty work.

The next morning at the Dollar Store I grabbed a case of tissues and thought to myself, "If one box is worth an extra point, why not get a case?" I shoved the boxes into the car and raced to find a Stella dress. After five stops, Eureka! I found a gauzy white sleeveless dress with a tiny belt that somewhat matched the photo I downloaded from the Internet. All that was left to do was make brownies.

Two days later, my son jumped in the car. With a smile he announced, "It was too late to get extra credit. The boxes were due yesterday. You can keep the Kleenex."

And my daughter's speech was canceled.

Twenty-four hours later I'm stuck with a case of cheap tissues, a dress to return, and Stage Two—Anger.

At Starbucks on the last day, the mood among the mothers was one of general relief. We vowed that next year we would do less for our kids, encouraging them to be empowered. No more last-minute trips to the school to drop off missing homework or library books. Forget about writing excuses for late passes. Stop making last-minute runs to the store for school projects. With a high-five, we declared enough was enough.

Stage Three—Bargaining.

The buzzing of my cell phone broke the jubilant mood.

"Hey, Mom. I left the brownies at home. Could you just run them up to school? Class starts in ten minutes."

"Sorry, I'm too busy," I said with a puff of my cheeks and a shoulder shrug.

"But, what do I tell my class?" she pleaded.

"Tell them you forgot. Gotta go," I said, and just like that I hung up. I've arrived at Stage Four—Acceptance.

I decided to eat the brownies. They tasted delicious.

STELLA!

COLD NOSE, WARM HEART

For her 14th birthday, Ashley welcomed Stanley, a nine-month-old white fur-ball puppy with slightly crossed green eyes. Destined for greatness, he had a natural good temperament and within a month he had mastered basic skills such as sit, stay, down, and leave it. He socialized well with cats and dogs in our neighborhood. Young kids loved him.

Ashley researched volunteer possibilities and discovered that her well-mannered pet would be a perfect match as a therapy dog to provide comfort and affection to people in retirement homes, hospitals, hospice, and skilled nursing facilities.

With a list of the requirements in hand, she set out to train Stanley. Crutches, wheelchairs, and walkers did not unnerve him. He allowed tasty treats to be removed from his mouth and didn't growl if we touched his food. He was on his way to passing the Canine Good Citizenship exam at the animal shelter. Test day arrived by summer's end.

"Think you're ready?" I asked.

"No problem," Ashley said, stroking his head. Stanley wagged his stubby tail and licked her hand in agreement.

He passed the fifteen steps necessary for certification and Tri-Valley Humane Society awarded him a purple vest embroidered with the title "Therapy Dog."

Ashley chose to volunteer at Roseview Assisted Living Facility. On our first visit, Gina, a slender, dark-haired coordinator, asked us to introduce Stanley to the residents in the common area, a spacious room with comfortable seating and a grand piano.

"Would you like to meet Stanley?" Ashley said in a boisterous voice to each resident. "Want to pet him?" Yesses echoed around the room and hands clamored to stroke his back or tickle his belly. They hugged and kissed Stanley, and he thanked them by sitting by their sides.

"What type of dog is he?" they asked.

"He's a cock-a-chon, cocker spaniel and bichon mix," she said with a satisfied smile. "Want me to put him on your lap?"

"Oh please," said a stout, cheery lady in two-piece pale blue jogging outfit, patting a spot on her lap. She stroked Stanley and he barked his approval. "He's so soft," she said. Her eyes sparkled. "Do I smell lavender?"

"I sprayed him with pooch perfume for his first visit," Ashley said. The lady crushed her nose into his fur; a contented smile warmed her face.

But we discovered that not everyone was receptive to Stanley's charm. "Get that dog away," said Alice, her mouth twisting and hands flapping. "I don't like them." Alice, a tall, loud talker, was disagreeable and short-tempered. Other residents avoided her. We spotted her staring at us from the corner of her eye as she kept a close watch on Stanley's whereabouts.

At our next visit, Alice sat alone in an overstuffed chair holding an AARP magazine in her lap. "Nice to see you again," Ashley said, taking a deep breath. When we sat down at her table, she made a sudden move to shift to her wheelchair and clutched the chair's arm with gnarled fingers.

"Can I help you?" I asked as I leaned forward and extended a hand.

"Not unless you get that ugly look off your face," she snapped.

What the hell?

"Hmmm, OK," I said, scratching my neck. *What now?*

Unperturbed by the rude comment, Ashley took Alice by the arm and guided her into her wheelchair. She hustled her back to her room, and I followed behind with Stanley on his leash.

On our way out, Stanley poked his head into Mary's room and she coaxed us into her studio apartment. Tiny and graceful, Mary treated Ashley like her granddaughter and called her Sarah. Stanley was mistaken for Samantha, the pooch she left behind when she entered Roseview.

"Come here, Samantha, you're so sweet," she said, holding out a crunchy peanut butter treat for Stanley. He lifted his paw for a shake. "Samantha, you're such a good dog. I missed you," she said. She cuddled Stanley and entertained us with funny stories, like the time her poodle ran away and ended up at the barbershop. After ten minutes, time for goodbyes; she shed tears when we left the room.

Our proudest moment came two months later, in the memory care area for Alzheimer's patients. In this section, the people were sedate and introspective, lost in their own imaginations. We suspected they might benefit from a visit from our Stanley.

We lugged a basketful of costumes for Stanley's fashion show. His outfits included a blue clown collar with a pointy hat topped with red pom-poms, resort wear, a leather biker jacket and a pink boa with matching tutu.

"What's your dog's name?" asked a lady stooped over in her wheelchair. She clapped in joy as Stanley strutted in a glossy rain jacket with matching boots. *I'm the bomb diggity*, he seemed to say as he swaggered past.

Patients who remained motionless during previous visits came to life as Stanley pranced by. He melted their anxiety, and both dog and patient enjoyed the physical contact. Now, despite their various stages of decline, most remembered their favorite dog and shared a little bit with us. They petted Stanley on their laps, sang, and laughed at his tricks.

"What's your dog's name?" asked the lady in the wheelchair again.

"Stanley," my daughter said.

"How old is he?" asked a disheveled curmudgeon.

"What's your dog's name?" asked the lady the third time.

Ashley repeated his name with the patience of a trained assistant.

Gina, our friendly coordinator, approached us as we left memory care. "You're doing a good job here," she said, squeezing Ashley's hand. "I've never seen them so animated. Thanks."

In the front lobby Alice intercepted us politely.

"Are you leaving?" she asked. "Did I miss the show?" Her eyes misted.

"We'll be back next week for another visit. You can help teach Stanley a new trick."

"I love dogs," she whispered.

WOULD IT KILL YA?

Don't get me wrong—I love being a stay-at-home mom. With a smile, I'll do laundry, prepare meals, vacuum, and even pick up you-know-what after the dog. But would it kill the rest of my family to help with household chores without all the whining?

One morning, my high school-aged daughter tapped a pencil fifteen times on the kitchen counter, sighed, and gripped her cell phone tight enough to lose circulation. This was her signal that she was ready to leave for school.

"Let's go, Mom," she said, while finishing a text message. "My friends are waiting."

I scanned the kitchen and spied her half-finished glass of orange juice, crusty bowl of cereal, and crushed napkin near her placemat on the table.

"Please pick up your mess," I said, wiping the counter with a dishrag.

My daughter remained motionless, except for her thumbs.

"Come on, Mom. We're late."

"Would it kill ya to put the dishes in the sink?" I asked, rubbing the back of my neck. "What's the big deal?"

After I got back home, I poured a cup of Joe and relaxed for twenty minutes—but it only felt like ten seconds. I peeked at the clock and realized that if my thirteen-year-old son didn't clean up, pack up, and hurry up, he'd be late for first period.

"Time to go," I muttered and grabbed the car keys. "Get your homework and meet me at the car."

I watched from the driver's seat as my boy exited the back door and ambled down the driveway, sluggish and drowsy, as though wading through Jell-O. With droopy drawers and downcast eyes, he dragged his feet the entire distance. I averted my eyes and laughed a little to myself. *How is it possible to move that slowly?* I thought. Earlier, he was riding his scooter and shooting basketball hoops at the same time.

"Would it kill ya to walk any faster?!" I cried out the window, placing my head on the steering wheel in mock frustration.

"I'm hurrying. Be right there."

"You're going to be late."

"Chill."

My expectations for my family are simple. Would it kill anyone to place scissors back in the drawer after using them? Put their shoes in the correct spot? Hang up a jacket? Be on time? *Am I asking too much?*

At dinnertime, I tried to squeeze out help with the evening chores. I craved spending quiet time with my husband before he dozed off on the sofa. If everyone pitched in, I wouldn't be stuck doing everything and we could all relax and unwind.

"Honey, please clear the table," I said to my son.

"Can you do it? I gotta go," he said, dodging eye contact.

"Go where?"

He tilted his head in the direction of the bathroom, "You know."

The bathroom faker.

"Would it kill ya to wait a minute? It's your turn."

"I'll be right back."

Bamboozled. A real Harry Houdini of the smooth getaway.

And a little personal grooming never hurt anyone either. After dinnertime, I snuggled by my husband's side on the couch. That's when I noticed a wiry gray hair poking out of the center of his left eyebrow. Like a thief, I tried to yank it out, but missed. After a few more tries, he begged me to stop.

"Would it kill ya to pluck that crazy eyebrow?" I said with a laugh. "It's blocking your eye." *Maybe I can tug it out in the middle of the night with tweezers?*

"Don't touch," he said, leaning away. "Trying to watch ESPN here."

"Please. It's so distracting."

"Leave it."

Finding it hard to focus on our conversation, I slipped out of the room to read *I Was a Really Good Mom Before I Had Kids*. In the den, my offspring stared at their respective computer and Xbox in high-tech trances. Unfolded laundry surrounded them like snowdrifts, piled high on every surface. I watched in awe as my daughter shoved the mass to the ground and plunked down her textbooks and backpack. My son took a novel approach and used the laundered clothes as a reclining chair.

Arrrrg!

"Would it kill ya to fold the laundry instead of pushing it around?" I asked with a weary shake of my head.

"We're tired," they replied in unison.

Exasperated, I rejoined my husband in the living room. But that rogue hair, which was as long as a pipe cleaner, still fascinated me.

"What?" I said. I was so mesmerized by the hair that I didn't realize he was talking to me.

"Do you want to go out to dinner tomorrow?" he said, apparently for a second time.

"Huh? I can't take my eyes off that hair. Pull it."

"Would it kill ya to stop saying that?" my husband said. He jumped off the couch and tried to hotfoot it out of the room. Not fast enough, I grabbed my man by the arm and held him in a warm embrace.

"I love you," I said, batting my eyes. Then with my thumb and forefinger, I quickly yanked that wild hair right out.

Score one for Mom.

STRESSED OUT IN THE PASSENGER SEAT

"Hurry up, Mom," Ashley yells. "I can't wait. I'm so excited! Are you?"

"Uh yeah. I'm ready," I stammer.

We hold hands as we walk towards the family van, car keys in my sweaty grip. The smell of freshly cut grass permeates the neighborhood. My feet begin to sweat and my lower eyelid twitches. It is time to give my daughter her first behind-the-wheel lesson. I feel like Tom Hanks in *The Green Mile*, going down that last stretch to the electric chair. I am not ready for this.

Despite my obvious apprehension, Ashley appears unaffected. She adjusts the mirrors with precision, scoots the seat back for her lanky legs, and tightens the seat belt. She shifts our Honda Odyssey into reverse, backs out of the driveway, and avoids the mailbox, the neighbor's Audi, and two kids on skateboards. She listens to my directions as I guide her out of the neighborhood and on to the main street.

I dole out driving wisdom as we approach the busy intersection, chock-full of honking cars. "Take it easy. We're coming up to a yellow light. Slowly push on the brake. Don't forget your blinker. That's it. Go slow."

She has done a great job driving, a perfect student. As for me, I'm a total mess. The steering wheel and brake pedal look miles away from my side of the car. I wonder how I ended up in the passenger seat. I stare at her shiny face and smooth blond ponytail and I remember.

It seems like last year I pushed her around in a stroller, marveling at each new thing she pointed at with her pudgy finger. Didn't I smile at the bravery she showed riding her first bike just last week? Wasn't it yesterday that she had her braces removed and laughed with glee as she rubbed her tongue around her smooth, straightened teeth? What is she doing in the driver's seat of our family van?

Jolted back into reality, I guide her back home. All aglow, Ashley parks the car in front of our house, pulls the key out of the ignition, and leaps out.

"You coming?" she asks.

"Be right there," I say. I need a few moments to compose myself after the lesson. Gripping the side door handle and pressing on an imaginary brake pedal takes a lot out of a mom.

Our next driving "opportunity" happens the following weekend. Like Pavlov's dog, each time Ashley hears the car keys jingle, she runs to the sound with a shout, "Can I drive?"

Running errands like grocery shopping or dropping off laundry, none of it matters to Ashley as long as she is behind the wheel. She manages the roundabouts and listens to my suggestions as she navigates through the neighborhood.

At the intersection, she approaches a red light. Since I want Ashley to make her own decisions, I remain quiet and wait for her to stop. And wait. And pray.

No indication of stopping whatsoever. My chest tightens, neck stiffens, and eyes blink.

"SLOWDOWN!" I say. "Didn't you see the red light?"

She turns to me and says, "I saw it. No problem."

My heart races and I try to refocus on her driving lesson, but what I really want to do is pull her out of the driver's seat by the ponytail and grab the wheel. My right leg buckles from pushing on a fake brake and my stomach churns.

"That's okay. Just try to pay better attention," I say. "You're doing great."

Ashley's driving no longer gives me facial tics or stomach cramps. Since the red light incident, she's hit a few curbs and a parking barrier but overall, she's a careful driver. My daughter is growing up and showing no signs of slowing down.

CHARITY AND THE CHUMP

In an attempt to teach my fourteen-year-old son about charity, I used every opportunity as a learning moment. He served meals at a food pantry in San Francisco, volunteered at Open Heart Kitchen and collected canned food for the needy. If there was a chance to help, he raised his hand.

Church needed volunteers at Glide Memorial Church in San Francisco, a community outreach program for those suffering from homelessness, hopelessness, poverty, and drug use.

He worked side by side with other volunteers serving meals and packaging box lunches. When he returned home, he relived his day with me and said, "We even ate lunch there. The food was a little better than yours."

Um, thanks?

He continued small acts of kindness. He opened doors for the elderly and helped seniors carry their grocery bags to their car. Then, late one evening, we stopped by Taco Bell for my growing son's fifth meal of the day.

A twenty-something homeless-looking man was sitting outside the front door with a sign. I explained to my son, "Here's what you should do" and handed him some money.

He approached the man and said, "Sir, would you like me to buy you something to eat?"

"No, I'm fine."

"Um, okay. Here, you can have this," he said and dropped five dollars into the homeless guy's jar.

At that moment, I reached the front door and squinted at his sign. *Wait a minute.*

"Can I take a closer look at your sign?" I asked. He held it in my direction.

"Are you kidding me?" I blurted out. "NEED MONEY FOR SCOTTISH FESTIVAL."

"Just trying to keep it real, lady."

Once inside, I discussed with my son the virtues of being honest. And the importance of reading carefully.

EXTREMELY LOUD AND INCREDIBLY CLOSE

Ever wonder if there's a surefire way to get your kids off the couch fast? Or move your husband? Just say you're going to take a nap. All hell breaks lose.

Let me start at the beginning. We enjoyed eating at Vic's All Star Kitchen on Saturday mornings. Nothing beat a big stack of hotcakes, thick smoky bacon, side of hash browns, and a plate of toast to induce a coma later in the day. By noon I could barely move, much less keep my eyes opened.

I said to my family, "I'll be upstairs. Taking a nap."

"Okay. Can I have some friends over?" my daughter asked, bolting off the sofa and stuffing a bag of popcorn in the microwave.

"Talk to your dad. I'll be in my room with the door shut. Try to keep it down."

Ten nanoseconds passed. My husband yelled from the bottom of the stairs, "Remember guys. Be quiet. Mom's sleeping."

Attempting to sleep here!

After years of trying to get my son to try piano and violin lessons, he tapped his way from the kitchen, up the staircase, down the hallway, and into his room with a pair of drumsticks that had been MIA for four years. Click, clack. My eyes fluttered opened like a moth around a porch light.

Not to be excluded, Stanley, the dog, expressed his displeasure regarding my nap as well. He sniffed under the door and catapulted his twenty-pound body forward. Ping. He gave me a smug look as the door burst open, then he routed in the blankets and staked out a comfortable spot at the end of the bed.

"Buddy, if you're quiet, I'll let you stay," I said, hopping up to shut the door.

What's that? A faint rustling of feet came from the staircase. Big man feet. Like a stalker, he paused, hesitated, and then ever so slowly turned the knob on the double doors. Kabong! Doors burst free. With a shuffle of sock feet, my husband whispered, "Don't worry. It's just me. I'll be done in a second and out of here."

Yeah, right.

After using the toenail clippers and electric razor, he stomped out of the room, pulled the doors shut and yelled downstairs to my daughter, "I'm on my way!"

I drifted off for a couple of minutes. From outside the opened window, I detected the whine of a chainsaw and the distinct smell of gasoline. When I married my husband, he was not a lumberjack. But Paul Bunyan decided to do a little light remodeling in the backyard. Now.

Oh, come on.

I popped up in bed, blinking like crazy. Out the window I spied a saw. And a tree. Timber. Next up, I watched as he reinstalled loose fence panels with a hammer. Bam, bam, buzzzzz. When finished, with a flourish he let out a big whistle for the kids to join him and admire his workmanship.

By that point, the dog couldn't contain himself. He charged the open window and jumped up and down to get a peek at the commotion. Ruff, ruff, growl.

Finally, I stuck my head out the window and said, "Hey!"

"Mom, did you get a good nap? Come on out."

Yeah, a full five minutes.

"Look what Dad just did. Isn't it great?"

"Looks fine. I'm coming."

If you can't beat 'em, join 'em. I'm going to sack out on the couch. Quietest place in the house.

WHAT WOMEN REALLY WANT

Mother's Day was always a big bust, and I was too exhausted to endure it again. This year I came up with a brilliant idea.

Two days before the big event, I prepared my answer to the question, "What do you want for Mother's Day?"

"Nothing," I said.

"Come on, we have to get you something. What do you want?"

"Nothing. I want a day filled with nothing. No fighting. No laundry. No cooking. No TV," I said.

"You're just saying that. You'd be mad if we don't get you a gift."

"Nope. This is what I really want."

"No way. That's too hard. Just let us get you a gift."

I stood my ground and reminded my family that I had been asking for nothing for years. I have suffered through pungent candles, perfume, glittery "Mom" necklaces and coupon books with sayings like "I'll do the dishes" and "Count on me to clean the house." Promises never fulfilled.

I explained to them that if they really wanted to get me the gift that I would appreciate and remember, it was the gift of nothing.

For the next two days, I did not hear a peep out of my family. I figured that they would do what they usually do, frantically shop for a gift at the mall or 7-Eleven the evening before Mother's Day. They would grab the first thing that they spotted, rush the cash register, and breathe a sigh of relief that their troubles were over.

But in the morning I was pleasantly surprised. I had dreaded the moment I would have to fake my pleasure at a potted plant or slippers. Again. But on the kitchen table was a card, signed by my husband, daughter, and son. That was it.

With a smile and a kiss, they said, "Happy Mother's Day. Enjoy your breakfast. We'll be upstairs doing laundry if you need us." I took a header into the scrambled eggs and bacon. Come again?

"Yeah, we want you to have exactly what you want, the gift of nothing," said my son, running off to join his sister.

Our house was as quiet as a funeral home—no shouting, no arguing, and no laughter. Everyone went about his or her business.

"I'll take the kids out of your hair. We'll be gone a few hours and bring you back lunch," said my husband.

Once the house was empty, I paced the kitchen, walking around in a circle like a caged animal. I plopped on the sofa. Turned the TV on. Turned the TV off. Is this what I wanted, a silent, vacant place devoid of noise and movement? Standing as rigid as a statue, I opened my mouth wide, outstretched my arms, and yelled a huge, "YESSSSSSSSSSSSSS."

With my newfound freedom, I stretched out like a cat on the sofa. All mine. I didn't have to argue with a kid to move over. I turned on Desperate Housewives extra loud and watched a full uninterrupted hour without having to re-explain the episode to my husband. I drank a milkshake without anyone grabbing the glass and slurping out of my straw. I read a *People* magazine and no one peered over my shoulder to ask stupid questions like, "Who is David Cassidy? " and "What is a Brazilian wax?"

After a few blissful hours alone, my heart rate went down and I smiled to myself, "Life is good."

Then I heard the slow hum of the garage door opener. Damn, they're back. Quick, I pretended to be asleep on the sofa. Rushing through the door, they asked, "Did you have a good day? Did you get some rest? Did you miss us?"

"Oh, I really missed you guys. It was so boring and lonely. What did you do?"

They shared stories of going to the movies and brought back In-N-Out Burgers for me.

"That sounded like fun. I should have gone with you."

And when they asked me what I wanted for Mother's Day next year, I said, "Three nights in Hawaii. Alone."

MR. KNOW-IT-ALL

Nothing is scarier than walking into your son's bedroom to catch him reading the Department of Motor Vehicles booklet. At that moment, I knew I had to find the Excedrin.

I hadn't reminded my son that he was approaching the eligible age to take the DMV test, because imagining him behind the wheel of the family van caused me stomach ulcers and nightmares. His personality was spontaneous, excitable, and emotional. And then there were the insurance issues. Teenage boys are considered careless drivers with out-of-control insurance premiums. *Maybe he could wait and get his license after he found a job or got married*, I thought.

"I want to begin my online classes," he announced one morning, spinning gum around his finger.

"It's too soon," I said. "You can't take the test until you're fifteen and a half."

"That's in two weeks," he replied.

Busted.

The next time he asked, I tried the Stupid Mom approach.

"I want to start my online driver's education class

today," he said as he tossed a cupcake into the air.

"Lost my Visa," I said. "Try again next weekend."

My procrastination technique sounded as weak as Lance Armstrong without performance-enhancing drugs. But I was terrified at the thought of him behind the wheel, unleashed on the world.

My son's ideas of car safety rival the two-day vacation-turned-nightmare in the movie *Thelma and Louise*. For example, as I drove home from the mall, the streetlight turned green, yet the car in front of us remained stationary.

"Get real close and push him across," he said, irritation wrinkling his forehead.

Oh, crap! Did he just say what I thought he said?

And he did not seem to think the speed limit and rules of the road applied to him.

"Don't let that car beat you to the stop sign," he said in a loud voice.

Yowza!

Finally, I caved in to his request to start his online training. He was a man on a mission, a boy possessed. As he got closer to completing his online classes, his attitude got even worse.

"Ten and two," he said, glancing out the window.

"What?" I asked, peeking at him from the corner of my eye.

"Hands. Ten and two," he repeated.

"Thanks," I said, feeling as if I were the one about to take the driving test.

Ol' Eagle Eyes never missed a moment to remind me about The Rules. "Hey, you're blocking the crosswalk," he said during the drive to school, as he stared straight ahead. "One point. You failed the test."

And he caught every driving infraction. "You're going eight miles over the speed limit," he sternly warned.

"No I'm not," I said, pursing my lips. "This area is thirty-five miles per hour."

"You're not outside the school zone yet," said Mr. Know-It-All. "Two points off."

He provided public service announcements free of charge. "Did you change the address on your license yet? You need to do that when you move."

"Nah, too busy."

"It's a $500 fine and three points if you don't change it within ten days. You're breaking the law."

And he believed he knew all the shortcuts, too. "You're going the wrong way. Turn right, left, left, through the intersection and north on Highway 680."

A regular Rand McNally, I fumed silently. But at the same time, I was proud of my boy—he was really serious about becoming a good and safe driver. I was relieved that he had learned a thing or two.

"Are you listening to me?" he asked.

"Yes, dear," I said, smiling to myself.

He studied in the car, after school, at dinner, in the bathroom, at every available moment, intent on finishing his driver's test before he turned the magic age. Final online score: 89 percent. An official certificate arrived in the mail the next week. He circled the kitchen island, anxious to start his behind-the-wheel lessons.

"Ready to take the written test at the DMV?" I asked, grabbing the car keys.

"I'm ready," he said, hopping from foot to foot. "Do I have to pay for it?"

"Yep, that will be $50." *Or two points,* I thought to myself.

COLLEGE SEND-OFF

Ashley is our first-born, and my husband and I had documented all her firsts: first steps, first words, first day of kindergarten, first car, and now, first child to attend college. We recognized that everything we had done up to this point was practice.

Throughout the summer, we shopped together for college essentials like toiletries, colorful bedding, laundry baskets, eating utensils, and power cords. She selected her college courses online and searched for a roommate through the school's Facebook page. She was ready to begin a new adventure and had marked off the boxes on the college checklist.

As move-in day approached, I second-guessed everything. Should I have the big talk with her about binge drinking, campus hookups, and the importance of staying in groups? Can she manage money? Should I call, text, instant message, Skype, or email?

The night before move-in day, her dad returned from Home Depot with packing materials. He stacked the flat cardboard cartons, packing tape and packing paper in a neat pile in the garage.

"Okay, let's get started," he said to Ashley. "Assemble the boxes and load your stuff. We'll be pulling out early tomorrow to beat the traffic."

Ashley took one look at the stack then stared at me. I pretended to look away. *I know that look.* She scanned the area like an X-ray technician and tried to get eye contact from Dad.

After ten seconds she pleaded, "Can you guys help me?"

With a subtle tilt of the head, I pointed a finger at the back door and encouraged my hubby to meet me in the kitchen. "She's struggling with the tape roll," I whispered. "Should we help?"

"If she can't put together a tape dispenser, she's not ready for college," he said, raising his eyebrows.

For thirty minutes, she huffed and shoved her supplies into the bins, labeled them with the dorm room number and loaded them in our car.

Ta da.

We left our house for the college campus around 7:30 a.m. Student volunteers rushed our car with baskets to wheel her stuff inside. Each freshman was allowed one bin. Ashley filled three. *Surprise.*

We helped make her bed, hung a mirror, and taped pictures to the wall. Her roommate walked in and introduced herself. *What a relief. Looks like a good kid, no nose piercings, spiked hair or tattoos.*

After the space was somewhat arranged, Ashley asked, "What are your guys' plans?"

"Your father and I thought that once you're unpacked, we'd meet a few other parents from your floor for lunch."

"What?" she asked. "You're planning on staying? We thought the parents would be gone by then."

"Oh. I had no idea," I said, rubbing my hand through

my hair. "Thought it might be fun."

"The kids on our floor planned to hang out," she said.

"Now what should we do?" Mike asked me.

"Well, I guess we'll bring up the rest of the cartons and then leave."

Drop-and-dump method.

"Oh my gosh. Just treat me like luggage. This is so sad. You're ditching me on my first day at college."

Huh?

We compromised and unpacked the last few boxes, gave her a final hug, and left. Looking over my shoulder, I whispered, "See you soon," then grabbed my husband's hand and strolled down the dorm hallway.

Our first-born baby girl is all grown up, off to college. It's time to say good-bye. Time to let go. Time to whisper, "I'll always be here if you need me."

And time for Mom and Dad to celebrate. Champagne, anyone?

HUNGER GAMES

Like wild animals underneath the Coliseum on game day, passengers queued up outside the cruise ship doors, anxious to attack the buffet. At that moment, I snatched my bags and eyed the exit. Would I be able to resist the lure of food for ten days?

Dear God, grant me strength.

My family of four, two teenagers in tow, cruised the Baltic this summer and my only concern was the unlimited opportunity to eat twenty-four hours a day. Upon embarkation, our captain bellowed across the speakers, "During the boarding process, only the lido buffet will be opened, located on deck number nine." Fifteen hundred shipmates charged.

Food vied for our attention, ranging from tempting cheesy entrees to tasty sweet snacks and to-die-for desserts like delicate cream puffs and cherries jubilee. I hadn't seen this much grub since the Biggest Loser temptation challenge.

At this point, my reserves started to melt. We fought through the crowd. Geez, it had been a whole hour since we last ate.

Oh boy, I'm starving!

The lunch banquet glittered like the Hope Diamond and beckoned me closer. A voice inside said, "Go ahead. Take all you want. Pile it to the sky."

A rookie mistake.

I overloaded my plate. At home, I'm conscious of fat and carbs and do a good job balancing my food intake. On board, I'm as weak as Superman with kryptonite.

Day two at sea, I wore my stretchy pants. First decision of the day, breakfast. As I reached the buffet, I admired the elegantly carved watermelon with fruit as flowers.

What the heck? Get that crap out of the way! It's blocking the good stuff.

"Good morning," said the server, eager to dole out gigantic portions of hot, cheesy omelets, sausage, hash browns, buttery croissants, and Belgian waffles. I sampled it all.

Later, my gang roamed around the ship, played shuffleboard on deck, chilled out on lounge chairs. And what do you know? It's lunchtime! We picked baked ziti, spaghetti, ravioli, garlic bread, and a side salad. I pushed the salad off to make room for a cookie. I'm on vacation.

After a two-hour nap and quick shower, we headed to formal night in the main dining floor. Seafood Extravaganza.

Tall and lanky, sporting a wide smile, our Indonesian head waiter, Agung, asked, "Sir, for starter, you like shrimp cocktail, fresh fruit medley, or gazpacho soup?"

"All," said my husband.

When he recovered, he continued, "For main entre, I offer steak or lobster. Very good."

"Uh...both," my husband said, looking a tad embarrassed.

By dessert, I released my belt a few notches and thought, "Just a bite never hurt anyone."

"Madam, what can I offer for dessert?" asked Agung, anxious to please in his black tie and jacket.

"Can you bring me the crème brûlée? And would it be possible to sample a piece of the molten lava cake and a tiny cream puff?" I grimaced as I pulled on the elastic band around my waistline.

"As you wish."

At bedtime, the massive overeating continued.

"Mom, can I call room service? Still hungry," said my son, wide awake and ready for more.

Why not?

Our room server delivered cold milk and soft-baked chocolate chip cookies to the kid's cabin. They passed out around one a.m. in a hazy, sugary, carbohydrate overload.

Thankfully, day three was our port of call in Russia. Walking around would burn the calories we needed to break even on calorie consumption. We toured the Hermitage, Catherine the Great's Winter Palace, the Cathedral of Saints Peter and Paul, and the Church of Our Savior on Spilled Blood. Despite all the splendor, we couldn't take our mind off the cruise food.

Back on the ship, we assaulted a dinner of wild mushroom cream soup, grilled red snapper fillet on gazpacho juice, and Grand Marnier soufflé. Afterwards, I endured a bellyache and massive gas pains. Like my Samsonite luggage, I possessed handles.

Our eating frenzy continued through days four and five.

By day six, I paused on the lido deck and said to myself, "Step away from the buffet." I grabbed oatmeal with a small serving of dried fruit and let out a low belch.

With four days left, I attempted to return to my pre-cruise weight before we disembarked The Fat Boat. Seasoned cruiser Marge gave me this advice: "Honey, you need to drink lots of water to fill up. Avoid hot foods for breakfast. No snacks between meals. Be wary of mixed drinks. Don't eat salty foods. Take the stairs when possible. Exercise in the gym. Run on the track. Eat more salad."

Bye-bye, stretchy pants.

THE REWRAPPER

~~~~~~~~~~

As Christmas barreled towards me like a supernova, my armpits got as sweaty as the Shoe Bomber going through customs. My fear? Receiving a present that I disliked and having to fake my approval. Opening a gaily wrapped box with yards of ribbon heightened my anxiety to Code Red.

Last Christmas, my family watched with bated breath and I tried to camouflage my true feelings.

"Oh thanks. What is it?" I said.

"It's that thing you asked for," said my son.

I didn't have a clue if this was something I had wanted as a gift. I understand that I'm difficult to buy for at birthdays and holidays. I don't wear a lot of jewelry. I have bottles and bottles of perfume on my bureau that I do not use. Don't even think about buying me clothes, flip-flops, a whoopee cushion, a low-fat cookbook, or a hermit crab.

In order to avoid hurting people's feelings, I started a practice I am ashamed to admit: I unwrap my gifts before Christmas and then rewrap them before getting caught.

You've heard of the Regifter, the guy who has the

nerve to recycle your gift by giving it to someone else? I call myself the Rewrapper.

I have pinpointed the exact moment my rewrapping habit started, a birthday celebration ten years ago. It was a typical party, cake, ice cream, "Happy birthday to you," the works. But as my family gathered around in a circle, my husband hoisted a medium-sized box in the air. Panic.

With a huge smile, my husband placed that box into my lap as my family looked on with glee.

Hmm, it had some weight to it. Please God, don't let it be a statue.

Sweat trickled down my side. Rapid blinking.

"Well, what are you waiting for? Happy birthday," he said.

I unwrapped my gift with the precision of a surgeon, trying to drag out the inevitable. Inside the box was a bronze statue of a nude couple in an erotic embrace. What the hell was he thinking? It was downright pornographic.

"Hmmmmm…thanks?" I said.

"Don't you love it?" he asked, searching my face. The rest of the family froze.

"Oh sure. Sure. I have the perfect place in our room for it." I snatched the statue and rushed out, faking a bathroom break.

That moment I transformed into the Rewrapper. I couldn't risk hurting anyone else's feelings ever again. Now, before any occasion that involves the exchange of presents, I take a peek at the present beforehand and rewrap it. The gifts I have received since then are as bad as ever, but I am prepared with a smile and a kind word. I say bring it on! I can muster a positive, heartfelt response to even the worst gift.

For instance, last year I received size 11 men's shoes from my husband.

"Thanks so much. I needed these." And a gift card to get a massage at the spa. The place had gone out of business. No problem. "I love it!" An industrial-sized space heater from my kids. "Fantastic!"

But this year there were no presents under the tree for me. What was up with that? "Merry Christmas," said my husband, "Here's a gift I know you will like," and he handed me cash.

Hallelujah!

THINK LIKE A MAN, BUT DON'T THINK TOO LONG

HE WHO KILLS WEEDS

~~~~~~~~~~

"If you're interested in keeping this job, you cannot speak to my husband," I said to Francisco, the new lawn-service guy. "If he asks you any questions, you must say, 'No hablo inglés.' Deal?"

"No problem. But why?" Francisco asked, scrunching his eyebrows.

"Do you have a minute?" I asked, rubbing the back of my neck and pointing to a folding chair. "Take a seat."

It all began eight years ago in Colorado. We used Crack-O-Dawn Lawn Service, but my husband, Mike, believed they were not doing enough to kill unwanted dandelions, daisies, crabgrass, and thistles.

Mike announced, "I'm going to Home Depot to buy some Ortho Weed-B-Gon." He grabbed the car keys off the kitchen counter and away he went.

"Wait. You have to take a kid with you," I said, picking oatmeal bits off my T-shirt with a fingernail. "They've been driving me crazy all morning."

On cue, our five-year-old daughter kicked over a stack of books and spilled apple juice on the tile floor.

"I want ice cream!" she demanded, hands on hips.

"No," I said, taking a deep breath. "We just finished breakfast."

"Chocolate ice cream with sprinkles!" she wailed, thrusting her head backward.

"No," I repeated for the tenth time. *Calgon, take me away*, I said to myself, dreaming about a long, hot soak in the tub with a glass of wine. Yes, I knew it was still morning.

Despite the kitchen chaos, our three-year-old son played with Duplo building blocks in the living room, quiet as a lamb. At least somebody was relaxed! He had no reaction to the conversation either way, but sweetly played with his favorite toys.

Mike's head swiveled between the kids—The Screamer and our son—just like a barn owl. He was trying to decide which one to take to the store with him. In a flash, he snatched our son off the ground, stuck him on his shoulder and headed for the door. My husband was no dummy. Our daughter's temper tantrums were legendary. She could hit decibel levels higher than the emergency alert system.

Mike returned home with his purchases and plunked our son in his crib for a nap. Then, with weed killer clenched in his sweaty fist, he scooted outside and attacked the lawn with the vengeance of Attila the Hun. For hours, Mr. Thorough sprayed the deadly weeds, vigilant not to miss a spot. Finally finished and pleased with his work, Mike showered and plopped in front of the television for a little R&R.

But in a few days, our lush, bright green Zoysia grass transformed into a smoky gray-green color and large patches turned sandy brown and crunchy. During his usual service appointment, Joe, the owner of Crack-O-

Dawn, rang our doorbell. "Lady, something's wrong with your grass," he said, shaking his head.

"Oh, don't worry," I reassured him with a toss of my ponytail. "My husband sprayed it good with Weed-B-Gon."

"It is killing more than weeds," he said through narrowed eyes. "Show me what he used."

I rummaged around in the garage until I found the spray bottle. Joe's eyes opened wide. "Did you read the label? This is bad. I've never seen it happen before." He paused. "Is he here?"

I hollered through the rear door for He-Who-Kills-Weeds to meet us in the garage.

The two of us stood with our heads down as Joe admonished us. "Sir, you used total vegetation killer, not weed killer. This stuff seeps into the area, 12 inches deep by 12 inches in circumference, killing everything in its way." Flipping a hand in dismissal, he said, "You'll have to dig it all out."

When Joe left, my better half crumpled into the reclining chair and said, "Never say a word about this to anyone. Promise?"

"No problema."

I won't tell anyone. I'll tell everyone.

Later that day, he shoveled dirt out of the affected areas. After seven days of excavation, our yard looked like the scene in the movie *Holes* where the juvenile detainees shoveled pits in the desert to "build character."

News of our predicament spread in our cul-de-sac as fast as gossip at an all-girls' high school. Neighbors sauntered past our lot with their small children and pets. I could almost hear them say, "That's the house I told you about. It's a real shame what happened."

It took two years for our lawn to recover, but my husband pinky-swore never to fertilize, aerate, kill weeds, or pick daisies again when we moved to our new home in California. "Look, don't touch" was his new motto.

When I finished my story, Francisco shrugged his shoulders, "Oh, this is the reason I can't talk to your husband?"

"That's right."

Years later, Mike still claims he made the "big mistake" because of our young son, who had distracted him that day at Home Depot, the day he bought the wrong product. I bet next time he goes shopping, he takes The Screamer.

TEA PARTY

~~~~~~~~~~~~~~~~~~~~

Blame it all on me. But in my defense, I didn't anticipate that my family would fight for iced tea.

First thing you need to know: my husband is a patient, reasonable man. He never gets mad over little things.

"What's for dinner?" he said, sniffing the air for a hint.

"Leftovers," I said as I turned on the microwave.

"Fantastic."

And after the meal, he asked, "Do we still have some of that chocolate raspberry truffle cheesecake from the Cheesecake Factory?"

"Oops, the kids ate it."

"No problem."

But if anyone messes with his iced tea, prepare for an all-out war brewed to boiling proportions.

There's a little story behind how it all started.

On my quest for a healthy alternative to soda and sugary drinks, I discovered caffeine free, no-calorie Crystal Light Iced Tea. My family fell in love with it, gulping down a gallon a day. Home from school, the kids downed it with their snacks. When the jug got drunk dry, the blame game began.

"How come the tea's gone? Who forgot to fill it up?" I said and shook my head.

Both kids denied that they had the last drink and refused to refill it. Sometimes the carafe was returned to the refrigerator with one inch left. Other times, it was put back completely drained. A standoff ensued.

After work each night, Big Daddy tossed his sport jacket on the nearest chair and marched to the fridge in search of his favorite beverage to guzzle. "You've got to be kidding," he said, shaking the container in our face, ready to blow. "Who forgot to refill this?"

Fee-fi-fo-fum.

We compromised. A black line, marked within four inches from the bottom of the container, represented the minimum fill line. Basic rule: if you poured below the mark, you refilled it. This worked for a while.

"Why's this so weak?" asked Mr. Thirsty. With an outstretched arm he flashed pale-colored tea in the glass pitcher. "Was it you?" he said, looking in my direction.

Me swill tea? My drink of choice —Pepto-Bismol, straight from the bottle.

Outwitted by teenagers again. They had filled it up to the top with water in order to avoid making a fresh batch. When my daughter confessed to the crime, I put a circle with a slash through her name on the pitcher. Banned until further notice.

Next day, I heard the garage door open. Daddy's home. The teens had chucked a pile of school stuff at the backdoor: backpacks, shoes, sports equipment, and cleats. He stepped over the junk and nudged a soccer ball across the room, but in the kitchen he exploded. "How come the pitcher on the counter is empty? This is ridiculous!"

Take it easy, Crazy.

"Calm down. I have an idea," I said before his head popped off. I grabbed another pitcher and marked on the front, in enormous letters, "DAD."

Total tally, two jugs.

But they couldn't resist one final swan song. The kids gawked with glee as Dad filled his jug to the tiptop and strolled away with a smug look on his face. As he turned the corner, I stared as the kids emptied the "DAD" jug into their own. Can't wait until he gets thirsty.

BARBECUE LIKE A MAN

My husband decided that the first day of summer was the perfect opportunity to teach to our teenage son the finer aspects of barbecuing. I spied through the mini-blinds in amusement as they walked in unison to the silver behemoth in the backyard, the Grillmaster 5000.

My man raised the lid with as much reverence as the scene from Indiana Jones when he uncovered the Ark of the Covenant. Brown, crushed leaves and nine month's worth of dried bugs exploded out the top.

The Master and Teenage Apprentice spent the next thirty minutes with their heads deep within the confines of The Grill. Dad gestured with an eighteen-inch, professional-grade stainless steel spatula. Step-by-step he instructed our son on the proper way to cook slabs of ribs, tri-tip, sausage, and chicken. They smacked their lips as dreams of blackened beef, fowl, and pork brought drool to their mouths.

The Master taught the teen the correct ways to flip the meat using chef's tongs, a two-pronged fork, and proper basting techniques. "One and a Half Men" joked, shot basketball hoops, petted the dog, and lounged poolside with cool drinks. Together they waited. And stared. And waited. And waited.

I, on the other hand, remained cloistered in the kitchen and prepared the rest of the meal. I stuffed deviled eggs, baked sweet potato fries, chopped, diced and sliced vegetables, tossed a Caesar salad, buttered garlic bread, set the table, poured drinks, and ran five loads of laundry.

An hour later, like Simba's presentation ceremony in the *Lion King*, my guys handed me a heaping platter of smoky, charred delights.

"Here you go, Honey. Hope you enjoyed your night off from cooking," my husband said, chest out and face beaming. "You're welcome."

DADDY DIVA

Staying on a diet is difficult, but living with a dieter is even harder.

My husband's weight had edged upward for the last year, and at night he sounded like he'd swallowed a party horn. I endured his snore fest for a year and then gave an ultimatum: "I'm going to sleep in the other room," I said. "Can't take it anymore."

He squished his eyebrows together. "What are you talking about?"

"Your snoring. It's got to stop," I whined. "Haven't slept well in a year. I'm a walking zombie."

"I don't snore," he said, raising his voice.

"Here's proof," I said and held my iPhone in front of his face. His eyes widened as he watched his slackened mouth whistle, snort, and wheeze. Despite the evidence, he denied having a problem and fell back asleep.

Months later, when he divulged to the kids and me that his belts were too tight, he admitted he might have a weight problem. He discovered an iPhone application called *Lose It*, designed to help the user stick to a weight-loss plan.

He entered each bite of food into the app, input the

codes from food packaging, and recorded the quantity. Zap! It computed his caloric intake. He didn't eat a meal without checking *Lose It* first.

Annoying.

We used to select our meal choice from the menu at our favorite date-night restaurant within a few minutes. Bing, bang, boom. Now it took my husband as long as reading a James Michener novel to place his order. "Are you ready yet?" I asked him as I jiggled my foot and gazed around for the server.

"Not yet. Need to check with *Lose It.*" He flipped through the menu and posted all the possibilities into the app.

More like the Food Nazi.

Ten minutes later, *Lose It* voiced her approval and my hubby ordered pasta with marinara sauce, a lettuce salad with balsamic vinegar dressing, a tiny chunk of French bread with light butter, and a glass of water.

After dinner, I suggested, "Hey, let's get Starbucks."

"First I have to check and see if I have any calories left for the day." He parked the car and typed away.

I envied couples that strolled into the coffee shop and shuffled back out with hot coffee. I steamed in the passenger seat as he tapped in a whole day's worth of meals.

"Do you remembered what I had for breakfast?" he asked.

I barely remember what I ate an hour ago.

"Pancakes?" I replied.

"Now I remember, cereal. Wanted to save calories for supper."

He plunked into Food Nazi: one-cup Cheerios, half a cup of milk, small piece of banana, and coffee.

"Did I drink more than six ounces of orange juice? What was for lunch?"

Are you kidding? Maybe there's an app for memory loss.

Twenty minutes later, he finished registering an entire day's worth of calories just as the lone barista locked the front door. Closed for the evening.

Bye-bye, latte.

For four months, my husband showed a determination unparalleled by previous weight-loss attempts. I got used to *Lose It* as a constant companion and no longer minded waiting to place an order at a restaurant.

His clothes loosened and he had a spring to his step. He felt good and it showed. "You're looking good," I said. "What your secret, Sexy?"

"Just trying to eat right, check the carbs, and calories. *Lose It* really works."

But things got tougher as he headed toward the final stretch. It was getting harder to lose the final five pounds, and he was off his regular schedule. At the airport on our way to a family vacation, my husband handed $50 to the kids to buy snacks for the whole family. He rarely gets frazzled or raises his voice. But that day he was on edge.

Our kids jogged back from McDonald's. They handed Dad a kid's meal and small drink. "What's this?" he asked with a shake of his head.

Oh no. Here it comes.

"You know I can't eat this," he said, pointing at the white bag. "And is this iced tea?"

"Nope, Diet Coke," said my son. *Lose It* says Diet Coke is a big no-no. It sabotages a dieter's efforts by causing them to crave more.

"*I can't drink diet soda.*" He stood up, slam-dunked the soft-drink cup into the nearest trash bin, and marched away.

"He's such a diva," said my daughter, rolling her eyes.

"Leave him alone," I whispered. "He needs our support."

Four weeks later he reached his goal weight. And I deleted the Food Nazi app.

BIG SHOW-OFF

If I had known twenty-five years ago that my future husband was as uninhibited as Lady Gaga, I might have hesitated to take our dating to the next level. I knew he was funny, dynamic, and enthusiastic, but nothing could have prepared me for one evening's revelations.

Once Mike bagged a paying job in college, we were finally able to go out on our first real date, one that required more than five dollars. We shared a similar sense of humor and picked the Funny Bone Comedy Club.

Cutting our way through the smoky and congested entryway, we snagged a cocktail table a few rows from the stage. "Let's sit here so we can be close to the action," said Mike, swinging his legs off the barstool.

Lights flashed as the emcee paraded on stage. "Great crowd we have tonight," said a short, stocky guy with a booming voice. "Your evening's entertainment is renowned hypnotist, Bill Sandman. Let's give him a big round of applause."

Bill Sandman leaped onto the stage and the place went wild. After the applause died down, he explained that the evening's show used audience volunteers.

Twenty extroverts jumped up.

"You should try it," I said with a tiny nudge to my boyfriend. With nary a glance backward, he sprinted up to join the others on the platform.

Wow, that was fast.

The hypnotist instructed the participants to stand, arms at their sides. He paced like a panther across the stage, speaking in soothing tones. "Listen to my voice. When I touch you on the head, fall forward into my arms." Bill tested them one by one for their level of concentration, trust, and relaxation.

Bill said, "If I tap you on the shoulder, that means you're dismissed. Please go back to your seats." He excused most of the volunteers until six remained, three women and three men, including Mike.

Bill announced with dramatic flair and a wide grin, "Here are your stars for the rest of the night." Big applause erupted as the alcohol took a firm hold.

Once the volunteers were seated, Bill said, "Each time I say 'sleep' you will fall deeper and deeper into a hypnotic state. Your body will become very calm. Fifteen minutes of relaxing is equal to five hours of natural sleep. At the end of the show you will feel happy, positive, confident," he said in tones as smooth as buttercream frosting. "Give yourself permission to be really outgoing tonight."

Oh boy, this is getting good.

Like a mischievous puppeteer, Bill controlled his subjects. Under his spell, postures slackened, shoulders slumped, heads drooped, and legs loosened. Mike sagged in the chair like a wet noodle, his head rested against the wall and a smile curving his lips. Meanwhile, waitresses doled out mixed drinks to the sold-out show.

For the first skit, the hypnotist told his protégées, "You are in the most amazing orchestra in the world. When the curtain goes up, I want to see your greatest performance."

Mike rocked out in his chair, shaking side-to-side as he strummed an imaginary electric guitar fast and furious, like Eddie Van Halen. He shouted out the vocals of "Hot For Teacher" loud and proud. Other volunteers could not compare to Big Show-Off as they mimicked playing drums, piano, or cymbals.

"Sleep," Bill instructed with a playful grin. His dutiful servants slackened in their chairs.

"Now you are in the second grade. When the teacher's back is turned, make funny faces," he said. "When I count to five you're wide awake. One, two, three, four, five."

Big Show-Off tugged on both ears, stuck out his tongue, and rocked his head back and forth.

Nah-nah, nah-nah, boo boo.

"Uh oh, she's looking," the hypnotist said. Mike twisted around in his seat, hands in his lap. A regular Goody Two-shoes.

"When I count to five you will be wide awake and your proper age. One, two, three, four, five."

Bill continued to put the volunteers in and out of sleep. His marionettes smoked fake cigarettes, tickled each other with imaginary feathers, played cowboys and Indians, and discovered lost bellybuttons. With constant commands of "sleep," his instructions were obeyed. He owned them for the next hour.

But the best was yet to come.

Bill set up the final skit for the volunteers as they slept. "When I wake you up, the guys are going to be exotic female dancers. The women will be men enjoying the show. On the count of five, wide awake, everyone. One, two, three, four, five."

As their eyes blinked open, Bill said, "Introducing the finest exotic dancers in the world." Blaze and Gypsy were introduced and shimmied across the stage, much to the delight of the audience. "Last, but I'm sure not the least, the very sensuous and the slithery," teased the hypnotist. "She's evil, she's mean, and she's bad. She's the kinky Slinky."

Mike strutted on stage with a sneer and jiggled to the whoops and whistles of the fans. Like Charo, the Spanish-American actress and flamenco guitarist, he shook his rear in the faces of the ladies. He unbuttoned his long-sleeved shirt and threw it to his admirers. Next, he teased the "men" as he removed his undershirt and flashed his chest. One woman in the audience cheered and put a dollar bill in his pants, and Big Show-Off blew a kiss to the onlookers.

Cuchi-cuchi.

As the audience was being worked into a frenzy, the older lady on stage yelled, "I like Slinky," and covered her face with her hands in embarrassment. People whistled and encouraged him to "take it off."

This date was more than I bargained for. *Dear God*, I thought, *he's going to take it all off.*

At that point, with the crowd's encouragement, he cavorted and threatened to strip with a come-hither look and a wag of his finger. Bill asked him to take a seat, waltzed over, brushed his hand down the front of his face, and said, "Sleep." Mike leaned his head against the wall, closed his eyes, and passed out.

Whew, that was close.

As the show wrapped up, Bill waved his hand in front of the rest of the participants and said, "All of you, sleep." In one motion, everyone passed out.

"In a moment, you will be back to normal. You enjoyed your sleep. You'll feel wonderful the rest of the night. Since we are friends, you will do one more thing. After you are back to your original seat, when I say 'goodnight' you will say, 'God bless you all.' And only then you are free. You'll be wide-awake at the count of seven. One, two, three, four, five, six, seven."

Back at his chair next to me, Mike stared glassy-eyed at Bill. I asked him, "What do you feel like? Did you know you were up there for two hours?" But his eyes did not waver from Bill's face.

Bill thanked the band, the emcee, and the volunteers. Then, "You were a great audience. Thank you. Goodnight."

Mike and the others stood up on cue and shouted, "God bless you all."

I thank God that Facebook and iPhone had not been invented.

WAR IN THE SKIES

Flying has become tortuous since the advent of X-ray body scans, flight cancellations, smaller seats, and lost luggage. We travelers are sometimes treated worse than cargo.

But there are strategies to employ in order to survive flying. Southwest Airlines offers an open-seating policy where customers can grab any unclaimed seat. On a recent flight from San Jose to St. Louis, I hatched a scheme. I waited for my number to be called at the terminal, rushed to the first available empty row, and grabbed an aisle seat. Then I set a trap like a spider to solicit a seatmate.

Anyone who was skinny, without kids or a large handbag, and who appeared germ-free met my prerequisites. I spotted a possibility and announced to her in a loud voice, "Excuse me. Would you like to sit here?"

"Oh thanks. How thoughtful," she said. More like self-serving. But on airlines with assigned seating, your seatmate is a crapshoot. Take a recent Delta flight. Without checking my ticket, I was confident I was in the right row and grabbed a prized aisle seat. I stowed my books, attached the seat belt, and waited. And watched.

A rather portly man came barreling down the aisle, eyeing my area.

Oh God, please no. Just keep walking, I thought. Let's just get it out here—a one-size seat does not fit all. He lumbered by.

I survived the next wave of crying kids, sneezing teenagers, and businessmen with briefcases. A slim, petite woman smiled in my direction. Jackpot, come on over. She fumbled to check her ticket and said, "You're in my seat." I checked and rechecked my ticket. She checked hers again. Damn, I had the wrong seat.

I returned to the main aisle and moved down a few rows. Built like Dwayne "The Rock" Johnson, a man over six feet, four inches and 250 pounds was in the aisle seat of my row. I squeezed past Big Guy, climbed over his huge shoes, oversized coat, bulging briefcase, and big bag of greasy takeout food. I avoided eye contact out of pure irritation.

Then the flight attendant announced, "Put away all electronics. Buckle your seat belt."

Mr. Big dug around his seat searching for the belt, knocking me in the chest with his mammoth elbow. "Sorry. Can't find the darn seatbelt."

A few more jabs to my ribs and the search was over. I glanced out of the corner of my eye to watch him buckle in, no seatbelt extender necessary. Whoosh, like a can of biscuits, flesh exploded over and under the armrest and filled in all available spaces.

After removing his shoes and stuffing the extra blanket under my footrest, he asked, "Honey, could you please turn on the overhead light?"

That was his opportunity to snatch my armrest. My skinny arms were no match for his muscular, oversized appendages. I tried to ignore my discomfort and took a short nap. When I awoke, I discovered my tray table down, crowded with a cup of water, a can of soda, a coffee mug with the contents half finished, and *The New York Times*. An iPad was squeezed to the side, the cord dangling across my lap.

I let out a sigh and fought to keep my mouth shut. Despite its size, the tiny bathroom would be a welcomed reprieve from the cramped setting.

"I need to go," I said and rolled my eyes as he removed all his items from my tray table. Then he stood and let me by.

Over the loudspeaker, the flight attendant said, "Due to turbulence, you'll need to return to your seat, please."

You've got to be kidding.

In my hurry to be reseated, Big Guy moved to the middle seat. Despite his "nice" gesture, sitting in the aisle seat proved as bad. He leaned on me the rest of the flight, bending my spine like a case of scoliosis. I was so far into the aisle my head got clubbed by the drink cart.

Soon our captain announced, "Prepare for landing."

Once on the ground, I gave Big Guy a smooch on the lips. Then I whispered in my husband's ear, "Thanks for the terrific vacation," squeezed his arm and motioned for our kids, who were seated in another row, to wait for us at the exit.

Maybe next time I can be upgraded to first class.

TOMFOOLERY

"Got ya!" I said, bursting into laughter outside Principal Smart's office in high school.

"What the heck?" said my best friend Jackie, grabbing my arm and shaking her blond ponytail as she exited the office. "You got me good."

Jackie had fallen prey to my annual April Fool's prank. That year I wrote a note on the principal's letterhead: "Immediately report to the office by second period for disciplinary action." The English teacher, in on the joke, handed it to her during journalism class. Jackie's dazed look was unforgettable and motivated me to pull pranks every year.

In college on April Fool's Day, I nailed classic shenanigans—planted a shock pen on my friend's desk, cranked up the volume on a clock radio at 5 a.m., even pretended to be a teacher calling to cancel a test.

Once married, my husband and two young kids were the victims of my high jinks. The goal was to illicit milk-out-your-nose laughter. Golden-brown chocolate chip pancakes made with salt was a classic. Our seven-year-old daughter skipped to the breakfast table.

"Oh boy, yummy pancakes," she said, covering the

stack with syrup. After one big bite, her back stiffened and she let out a yelp, but then realized that her little brother hadn't tried a bite. She zipped her lips and stared at him, fork in midair.

As expected, my son stabbed a gigantic piece, stuffed it into his mouth. "YUCK!" His chair toppled as he galloped around the center kitchen island, face red and contorted, searching for a place to spit.

As they grew older, the April Fool's antics became more intricate. We created fake food like "mashed potatoes" using whipped cream, stuffed shoes with newspaper, sewed underwear together, or short-sheeted the beds.

My husband and I pulled elaborate tricks on friends and family. The key to the successful delivery of a prank involved knowing our victims' routine.

Our friend Scott told us that his wife hit a deer on a country back road driving home from work. We quizzed him for all the details in order to set the trap. Then we asked him to make sure Sandy answered the phone the next day.

"Mrs. Smith, this is Officer Smedley with the Fulton County Police," said my husband over the telephone, using his best impersonation of a Southern accent. "I understand you hit a deer yesterday on U.S. Route 19 around 7:00 p.m."

"Um, yes," said Sandy, clearing her throat.

She sounded as nervous as a pig at a barbecue.

"I'm sorry to inform you, ma'am, but per Georgia code, you are wanted for arrest due to the abandonment and mistreatment of animals, Article 1.2A. You must turn yourself in to the nearest police department by 8:00 a.m. and pay for cleanup." Then he added, with a sigh, "Was there any deer slobber?"

"Yes, there was slobber on the front windshield, but I thought the deer ran off."

"You're going to have to come into the station so we can get a good look at that deer slobber."

"Uh, okay," she said with a shaky voice.

Fearful that he may have gone too far, he said without the drawl, "Sandy, it's Mike. April Fool's!"

"Oh my God, I hate you!" she said with a gasp.

My gullible mother falls for our tomfoolery year after year. We've imitated annoying phone solicitors, angry bank tellers, and nasty customer-service reps. Thanks to us, she's almost fallen victim to a Visa scam, a towed car, and cheap home improvement.

But to date, all the hoaxes were mere child's play in comparison to my greatest prank, "Fake Tax Return." My mother had filed an early tax return and bragged about receiving a $350 rebate. On April 1st, I called her at work, pretending to be the IRS.

"May I please speak to Mrs. L?" I said in a nasally voice.

"Speaking."

"This is the Mrs. Crowley with the IRS. According to our records, you received a $350 tax refund. Unfortunately, due to a computer glitch, you actually owe $700."

"What? You've got to be kidding. No way," she said raising her voice.

"I'm sorry but the IRS needs to receive this immediately, otherwise you will pay a late fee. If you have any questions, call 555-1212."

I could feel the tension leaking through the phone lines as I prepared for an onslaught of uncontrollable rage. But before the situation got out of control, I shouted, "Mom, it's me." After all, the woman took meds for high blood pressure.

"You. Are. Kidding," she said with a small intake of breath. "Not again."

And I have next year's prank all lined up: a travel agent offering a free cruise. Happy April Fool's Day!

A MAN OF FEW WORDS

According to studies, a man speaks about 7,000 words per day and a woman uses 20,000. Need proof? Check out my guy's typical text messages.

Let me set the mood. It's around 6 p.m. on a Tuesday and I'm getting hungry.

"Are you coming home for dinner?" I texted, carefully spelling out each word with my thumbs.

"Ya," he texted back in a microsecond.

"What do you want to eat?"

"Anything."

"Okay, see you tonight."

":)"

See what I mean?

When it comes to using actual words in a live conversation, it's more of the same. But the moment I turn on a blender, dust buster, hair dryer, or hand mixer, he becomes a human magpie.

After breakfast, I ask, "What do you want to do this weekend?"

"Dunno," he says.

"Should we ask Mary and Frank over for dinner?"

"Hmmmm," he says, scratching his chin.

He's impossible.

Clenching my teeth, I pop off the sofa and turn on the vacuum. Vroom, vroom. Out of the corner of my eye, I sense movement. He's gesturing wildly with his hands and his lips are moving faster than the fan belt in our car.

In a garbled tone he says, "I thump ya wanna talka." He throws his hands up in the air and yells through the whistling of the vacuum, "Let's goa seep a movie."

You've got to be kidding me! I was sitting next to this man for over an hour. He mastered the one-word conversation, and now he has something to say?

"What did you say?" I ask, turning off the Hoover.

"Nothing."

GIRLS GOT GAME

Everything I needed to know about golf I learned from watching *Caddyshack*: it's OK to use explosives, cheating's normal, and kicking the ball can improve your score.

"Work's hosting a golf tournament this weekend," said my husband. "Wanna go?"

"No way," I said, shaking my head. "I need lessons first."

"Don't worry. It's a scramble," he said. "Players take their shot from the group's best ball."

Tee off time, Saturday, 8:00 a.m. sharp.

Already, I hate golf.

Immaculate lush green fairways graced the golf course. Maintenance crews mowed, raked, and cleaned up around the club. The moment we pulled our car into the entryway, an attendant dressed in whites grabbed the car keys, handed us bottled water, and pointed the way to our antsy group warming up on the putting green.

Gary, a pudgy thirty-something guy, swaggered toward us with his petite wife Susan trailing behind. Our partners had arrived.

"Nice to meet you," said Gary with a sneer. Then he turned toward his wife and yelled, "I bet you forgot the sunscreen and extra tees." A regular George Costanza from *Seinfeld.*

"Don't let him throw you off," my hubby whispered. "Just put the ball on the tee and take a gentle swing like we practiced earlier."

Practice? I guess he means the five minutes we warmed up. What's a tee?

His pep talk did little to control my nerves. I tiptoed up to the ladies' tee as instructed, set the ball on top, and with a whack, sent it flying with my Titleist titanium driver and a massive chunk of turf.

My body vibrated like vintage speakers screaming hard rock. "God, I nearly broke my arm," I said to my spouse, massaging my elbow. "What happened?"

"You hit the ground. Hard. Don't worry about it. Doesn't count."

I quit.

Our team schlepped through the golf course, the guys hitting and the ladies missing.

"Hurry up," Gary shouted at his wife.

"Sorry, I'm doing the best I can," she said in a slow drawl.

After a few more holes, Gary checked his Rolex and then nudged my hubby with his shoulder, "Hey, let's move on to the green."

You are ignoring golf etiquette. Wait till I take my turn.

My guy leaned over and said, "Don't worry about him. Just focus on your shot." Then he jumped in the cart with Rolex, headed for the green.

"Sorry about Gary," said Susan as the guys pulled

away. "He takes golf so seriously. Ignore him."

Gary started to putt before we could take our shots. "Go ahead," Susan said, motioning to me. "You're next."

"Shouldn't we wait until the guys finish?" I said.

"You'll never hit it that far. It's your first time golfing. Go on," she urged.

I looked straight ahead at the green, lined up my stance like my husband had instructed, and swung.

The ball took a high trajectory, soared in the sky, then arced downward. I tilted my head back to follow its path. Frozen in place, my mouth agape, I stared, unable to scream the warning.

Fore.

I drilled Gary in the center of his back. He wobbled for a few seconds then dropped to the ground, still gripping his putter.

Take that, you big jerk.

My husband jogged over and extended Gary a hand up. From a distance, I could see him convulse with laughter as he turned his body away from my unintended target, pretending to fix a divot.

I love golf!

GOING COMMANDO

Let's face it. Ladies' undergarments were not designed with comfort in mind. Not much has changed since the invention of the corset that was meant to give a woman an eighteen-inch waist.

But the undergarment I am going to rant about is Spanx, which closely resemble the old-fashioned girdle. They tout the motto, "No matter the occasion or season, we've got a shape to keep you looking great from all angles."

But at what price?

I heard of a case where the mother of the bride was stuck inside a full-body Spanx for five hours. If Spanx's motto is, "Spanx is here on your big day," where were they? It slims and lifts, but is it worth it?

My big moment to prove the claims made by Spanx finally came: my husband's company was hosting a New Year's Eve party and I needed a little tightening in some places, especially the tummy. At the mall, I purchased a pair of "Trust Your Thinstincts Mid-Thigh Control Panel Shapers" for $58. Size: large. Slimming level: medium. Unfortunately, I did not try them on in the dressing room before purchase.

Dress ironed, shoes polished, hair coiffed, face painted, it was time to get on the undies. Unwrapping the package, I realized I had made a terrible mistake. Straight out of the envelope, the pair that dropped into my palm was as small as a mustard seed. Were these for children?

The instructions or "warnings" stated that putting on Spanx was "moderately challenging." An understatement. Don't use after a shower. Use with baby powder. When all else fails, go up a size. Take your time. For additional assistance, call the Spanx hotline? Yeesh.

I stepped into the panties right-foot first, trying to pull up to the waistline on the first try. Major mistake. I was knocked to the ground.

Next, I entered the left foot. Starting from my ankle, I rolled a tiny bit upward. A combination of yanking, jumping, and holding my breath got the panties past my knees.

At mid-thigh, like a tourniquet, it was constricting and compressing my blood flow. As the panties climbed higher, I felt light-headed and sweaty. Losing circulation fast, I panicked.

It was time to call in the reinforcements. Or 911.

"Mike, help! I can't get up."

Rushing into the bathroom, he took one look at me on the ground, undies half-on, legs askew, and blanched.

"Avert your eyes," I said.

"Grab my arm. I'll try not to look."

I reached for his hand with a clammy palm. I realized as he pulled me upright that he may never look at me in the same light again.

"I'll be waiting downstairs," he said, blasting down the staircase.

Ping! One final yank moved the Spanx into place. But Spanx couldn't contain my fat any longer. It started to roll out the bottom and my knees grew as huge as my butt. Fat bulged above my waistline, yet not high enough to enhance the bust line. What do I do now, Spanx? Huh?

I threw on my clothes after molding the fat into the right places and then headed down the steps. Dear God, if this wrap-around dress comes undone, my husband will be lucky to keep his job.

At dinner, my stomach was compressed so tightly that I could only eat tiny portions of food. And drinking? Forget about that.

After three hours, I was eager to use the restroom. Twisting and turning in the confines of a bathroom stall, I made as much ruckus as a rugby player. I could dislocate a shoulder pulling my Spanx down.

"Are you okay?" asked the lady in the next stall.

"Just a little out of breath. I'll be fine."

After we left the restaurant before midnight, my husband said, "You seem happy. Did you have a good time?"

"Yep, it was fun."

Bottom line, stuffing Spanx into my purse and going commando was the only option. I value breathing and eating over beauty. My advice? Save the money and do sit ups.

FIVE MINUTES OF FAME

My husband lowered his briefcase to the tiled kitchen floor and flashed an oversized red, white, and blue envelope in my face. "Mark the calendar. We're going to a gubernatorial fundraiser next week."

"Sounds like a snore fest," I protested.

"We've got to go. My boss is hosting it at his house," Mike said.

I squinted at the invitation. "Will there be food?"

"For a mere $500 a person, we get to meet Governor Owens, and appetizers are included."

We're not experienced in the political scene, so I conducted a Google search to familiarize myself with the Governor's platform.

Based on his profile, he seemed a decent politician who made transportation, education, and tax cuts the focus of his governorship.

Good enough for me. I'm in.

In the weeks preceding the party, the evening news covered a sensational story about the Hayman fire, ninety-five miles southwest of Denver, the largest wild-fire in recorded history.

During dinner each night, we were glued to the

television. "Hurry, come watch," I said, grabbing my plate of spaghetti and plopping into the nearest recliner. "More coverage on the fire."

Tom Brokaw on NBC Nightly News questioned a local reporter at the site. "Bob, what's the latest on the Hayman fire?"

"This just in," the reporter announced. "Terry Barton, a forestry technician, is said to be responsible. Locals believe she set it on purpose to avoid having to fight fires in other states, enabling her to be home with her kids over the summer. She pleaded to receive less time and was given a six-year sentence in federal prison. Back to you, Tom."

"Can you believe that?" said my hubby with his fork held midway between his plate and face.

But I wasn't certain she deserved that much prison time. She claimed she had built a campfire ring to burn old love letters from her ex-husband. It sounded to me like the fire got out of control and she ran.

I'm fascinated with famous people, so I got to thinking. Maybe I could score some one-on-one time with Governor Owens during the party, with the Hayman fire as a talking point.

"Hey, I have an idea about the Hayman fire to discuss with the Governor," I said to my hubby.

And score a few points for myself!

"Go for it," he said.

I mentally prepared my shtick before the rally.

At the outdoor event, I scanned the area back and forth like a Secret Service agent. The Governor arrived with his entourage around 8 p.m. and our host said, "It is my privilege to introduce Governor Owens." The crowd broke into applause as he glided across a backyard the size of Comisky Park and mounted the steps to the makeshift stage, dark-haired and polished as a Hollywood celebrity.

Hello, Mr. Fortieth Governor of Colorado.

I pushed a few older folks out of my way on my quest to sidle up to him after he left the stage. My man followed in the chase, a reluctant ally. But, within ten feet, I froze, stared, and nervously scratched my nose.

The Governor glanced my way. Oh God, I just looked like I was picking my nose in front of Governor Owens. Okay, maybe he wasn't actually looking at me.

What's wrong with me? He's just a regular guy. Stay calm. Move forward.

I snapped out of my reverie as the crowd closed in, vying for his attention. I adjusted my skirt, smoothed my blouse, and walked straight toward him, a gal on a mission.

Then the unthinkable happened: like a shish-kabob skewer, my stiletto heel stabbed the American flag table skirt. It wrapped around my leg and held me in its grip like a viper squeezing its prey. Reaching down, I tried to shake my shoe free, tripped, and fell, dragging the linen and cocktail table with me.

"Oops, pleased to meet you, Governor Owens," I said, staring up at his extended hand as he reached down to help me off the lawn. I turned crimson from my cleavage to my face as I brushed the grass off my outfit.

"Are you okay, Miss…" said the Governor, waiting for me to identify myself.

What's my name? What's my name?

I blurted out, "It's Stacey. What do you think of the beautiful weather we've been having?"

What the hell was I saying?

"Yes, it's been nice," he said, gazing over his shoulder at other guests, plotting his escape.

Out of the corner of my eye I spied my husband's body shaking, holding in the laughter. Tears welled from the corners of his eyes.

"No, no, wait! I have a question for you," I said as I blocked his escape with my outstretched arm. "Would you consider letting Terry Barton do a public service announcement to reduce her prison time? A short message on radio or television?" I prattled on, my mouth moving as fast as a hummingbird's wings.

"Hmmm, that's something to think about. Nice meeting you," he said and strutted away.

His handlers escorted him in the other direction, in search of worthy donors.

My five minutes of fame, ruined.

"Mission accomplished," said my guy, pulling me in his direction. "You made an impression all right."

DOES SIZE REALLY MATTER?

Did you ever notice that the number of years you've been married determines the size of your mattress? When my husband and I were newlyweds, we slept on a double bed, kissing and hugging the night away, wrapped in marital bliss. Over time I realized a double bed was a colossal mistake, like sleeping in a crib with a hairy gorilla.

After ten years, we progressed to a queen and then a California king, the mother of all beds. With the extra inches we thought we'd have more room to stretch and stake out personal space.

"This bed is amazing," said my hubby. "Can't believe it took us so long to move up."

"I'll finally get some rest," I added.

Wrong.

I didn't anticipate the latest development that would keep us forever too close: a crater in the center of the bed as deep as a Florida sinkhole.

Like a magnet, each night I was pulled into that hole. It continued to grow and multiply in the middle of our giant mattress. My husband outweighed me. He must be the cause. Gravity pulled me downwards, closer to him. This raised several new issues.

Each night as he rolled nearer, my forehead broke out in beads of sweat as I anticipated what was to come. I stared at his shadow, outlined by the light through the window, and I stiffened as my body forewarned of The Elbow. As pointy as a Civil War bayonet, it tortured me with the accuracy of a Ginsu knife.

"Ouch, get that thing away from my face. Are you trying to blind me?"

He mumbled something that sounded like "shut up" and fell back asleep. In the dark, I contemplated my revenge. What type of person sleeps with their hands locked behind their head, putting an elbow in direct line with my eye? *Maybe I could poke him with my hairbrush to get him to roll over. Wrap him with electric tape to the mattress.*

Not only had The Elbow turned me into Swiss cheese, but my core temperature rose to dangerous levels due to his body heat, like getting too close to a pizza oven.

To maintain the distance I needed from the human fireball, I hooked my leg around the edge of the mattress and pulled myself to the side. That strategy worked some of the time. The rest of the time I woke in a sweaty mess on one half of my body. Worse than menopause.

Then there was the noise pollution. Endless snoring disrupted my shuteye like hard rock music. Snorts, gurgles, and whistles. The combinations were endless.

And even when he wasn't snoring, his heavy breathing was impossible to ignore. Air in through the nose, out through the flaring nostrils. In and out. In and out. In. In. In. Out. No particular rhythm. Even the dog jumped off the bed in search of some quiet.

But I vowed tonight was going to be different. I had

enough. Lying next to him, I could just make out my husband's face from the dim nightlight in the hallway. He slept like an angel, lips in a small circle, eyelids fluttering. Quiet for the first time in months. *I can't stand his breath in my face. Must wake him up.*

"Hey, Darth. Roll over, you're snoring," I lied.

After a year of restless slumber, back and joint pain, puncture wounds, and a melted face, I needed a permanent solution. Flipping the mattress might offer a slight improvement to the deep abyss.

According to the instructions, we flipped the mattress over and then rotated it 180 degrees. And that evening I prayed for blissful rest, a sleep so heavy that I would wet the bed.

But a new situation developed. In the low lighting, I noticed a giant lump the size of Mt. Everest occupied the center of the bed and caused me to roll off the side. I grasped my husband's arm across the bed to stay afloat.

In my frustration, I hopped off the bed, snagged a pillow and extra blanket from the linen closet, and headed downstairs. In moments, I heard shuffling footsteps.

"Why are you sleeping on the couch?" my husband asked, running his hand through his hair.

"More room," I mumbled.

THE UNIVERSAL WOMEN'S LAMENT

"What took you so long in the bathroom? *Anchorman 2* is about to start," said my husband, flagging me towards theater five. Oh, he wants to know what took me so long? Can he handle the truth?

At the theater entrance, I had told him, "I'll be right back. Gonna use the powder room. Wait here." I paused outside the ladies' room door. Twenty women lined up like soldiers, purses holstered, feet tapping out an impatient beat.

Memo to self, go before you leave home.

For men who haven't been paying attention, the line to the ladies' room can snake out the restroom, around the corner of the building, past the exit and through the parking lot. Gals go in pairs to have someone to wait it out with, like standing in line for Madonna concert tickets.

"Can you believe this? When are they ever going to learn? We need more bathrooms," said another lady in line.

"I bet it will be fast," I said, not believing a word.

Once I entered the actual bathroom, I checked underneath the cubicles for legs. Crouching down, one by one I made my way past three stalls. Occupied. Busy. Locked. Drats.

"What's the deal? Seriously, they need to fix this place," I said in a booming voice to the other ladies.

Bingo, a door opened. A lady bolted in front of me. "Please, can I butt? Can't hold it any longer," she begged.

"Sure, why not?" I said.

What's another hour and fifteen minutes?

I tilted my head at the sound of flushing. Me, me, my turn. The current occupant clutched her handbag and rushed the exit.

Save me a seat.

Once inside the stall, I realized that the lock was broken. And the purse hook missing. And the toilet seat covers gone. No toilet paper in the ladies' room, again.

Yowza.

I strapped my purse around my neck, held the bottom of the door closed, and squatted. Mother warned me to never, ever let my butt touch the toilet seat. I could catch a disease, be struck blind, get pregnant.

This awkward position put great strain on my thighs. I began to shake like an off-balance washing machine. My handbag slipped close to the commode. Then the unthinkable happened—my purse smacked the floor, the grossest place in the universe. As loathsome as a pile of manure.

And I still have to pee.

Next, the automatic sensor started flushing. A fine mist of water hit my back end, dribbled down my pants, and pooled on my sneakers.

"You've got to be kidding!" I screamed, banging my head on the stall wall.

"Are you okay?" said the lady next to me.

"Fine. Just fine."

I bent forward to flush the toilet again and pushed the door open with my rear, exposing myself to the others in line. *Avoid eye contact. Zip and flee.*

Purse encircling my neck, I reached my hands under the automatic soap dispenser. Empty. I inched my way down the row of sinks. Empty. Empty. Empty. Water will do. I snatched the one remaining hand towel. *This is not enough.* I wiped my hands on my pants.

An elegantly dressed woman and I exited the washroom at the same time. She had tissue paper stuck to her silk shirt and her boots were wet.

"Out of toilet paper? Use old Kleenex?" I asked.

"Yep, what happened to you?" she said, checking me out from top to bottom.

"Broken door lock. No soap."

By the time I tracked down my guy, half the Diet Coke was gone and the gallon-sized popcorn devoured.

"What the heck did you do in there? Write a novel?"

"Not exactly."

MAN VS. CHRISTMAS TREE

Our artificial, odorless, eight-foot-tall Christmas tree taunts us year after year. After a decade, assembling the three sections of the Rocky Mountain Pine is still as complicated as solving a Rubik's Cube. I fantasize dragging it to the nearest dump and lighting it on fire.

"Time to put up the tree," says my husband, grabbing the kids by the arm. "You want to help too?" he says, looking at me with squinty eyes.

"Nah, I'll just watch," I say.

I avert my eyes as my husband struggles with our tree like a wrestler performing an over-the-shoulder arm drag. Plunk. It hits the ground and green needles fall like dandruff.

This year more of the hinged branches snap and dangle downward. The razor-like needles draw blood on the family member willing to fluff and shape the tree. We plug it in, stand back and hold our breath, waiting to see if its pre-lit branches will shine this year. With a fizz and a pop, the top half burns out. Alas, the tree wins, mocking me with loose needles and faulty lighting. Again.

Burn, Baby, burn.

WHEN LIFE GIVES YOU LEMONS, THROW THEM BACK HARD

HAIR GONE WILD

Everything I needed to know about hair I learned from watching Charlie's Angels. They say that your favorite hairstyle travels back to the time when you thought you looked your best. For me that was the 1970s, and my hairstyle of choice was called the Farrah, after the late actress Farrah Fawcett.

The Farrah was a style I could figure out. Cool, feathered, moussed a mile high, curled up tight with an iron. I methodically worked on it each morning before high school, loading on gel, wax and mousse. I finalized the 'do with half a can of Aqua Net Hair Spray, thick and sticky. And I added a fake tan, orange streaks and all. Voilà, ready for school. The big hair look—no one could do it better than I could.

Forty years later, my Farrah style is still here, much to my daughter's dismay. She approached me in the bathroom one night as I was getting ready for date night with my husband.

"Mom, your hair looks so 1970s. Want some help?" she asked.

"I guess."

After having two children and lugging them around

to 2,890 baseball games and over 10,000 basketball practices for the last 17 years, I admit I've become a little lazy. I consider it fancy to put my hair in a ponytail and dab on lip-gloss. Who has time for a blow-dryer?

My daughter combed, twisted, teased, and sprayed my hair. After thirty minutes of grooming, she turned me around to gaze at her creation. I was at a loss for words. Lady Gaga stared back at me, with a quirky hair bow balanced on the top of my forehead. Add a meat dress and I would be unforgettable.

"I think I can handle it from here. Thanks," I said, as she walked out of the room.

Given the extreme distance between Farrah and Lady Gaga, I decided I needed an age-appropriate haircut, so I scheduled an appointment to update my look.

"What can we do for you today?" the gal at the salon asked as she pulled back my hoodie and yanked out the elastic band on my ponytail.

"I need an update. Surprise me."

"But what do you usually do?" she asked as she massaged my head with aromatic oils.

Oh, we don't want to go there. After Farrah, I went through more styles than Imelda Marcos has shoes. Remember the shag in the mid 1970s made famous by David Cassidy and Rod Stewart? Shorter at the top, downward layers in the front. Blow-dry upside down after loading on tons of styling gels, fluffy and full.

Or what about the perm? In the 1980s, I was treated to a home perm kit, courtesy of my best friends. Major frizz. Topped it off with an application of Sun In. Teased the bangs out, piled high with a scrunchie. I looked just like a poodle. Gob on gaudy jewelry to complete the ensemble. My friends and I looked identical.

Thankfully I never attempted the Dorothy Hamill or the female mullet.

My stylist tapped me on the shoulder to shake me out of my daze in order to witness her magic as she transformed my locks. For an hour she snipped and trimmed, paying careful attention to my face, hair texture, and lifestyle. She did an awesome job fixing my hair: smooth side-swept bangs and straight, glossy locks in the back. A natural look, I thought when I glanced at myself in the mirror. I liked what I saw.

"Thanks, I love it," I said with a hug.

I purchased all the hair products she recommended. "I can do this," I said to myself. Once at home, I darted into the bathroom to check it out in my own mirror. I admired the reflection staring back at me. But what if I just brushed a little here? Or curled a tiny bit there? Within moments, my hair was fluffed, poofed, and once again sprayed immobile. *Ah, much better.*

"Good morning, Charlie! I'm back. Miss me?"

HE'S NOT THAT INTO ME

Hiring a good handyman is as tough as trying to lick your elbow. Heck, finding my husband was faster, easier, and less expensive. Unfortunately, my husband doesn't do home improvement projects in his spare time. A combination of long hours at work and heavy air travel convinced him to leave home repairs to the experts.

After moving into a new house, I Googled "Handyman Services" and found match-ups like eHandyman. com and ChristianHandyGuy.com. I had to act fast. The twenty-year-old house we'd settled on was crumbling around us. We needed help before we had to sleep in a tent or move in with our parents.

Send me an angel, I secretly prayed to the home-improvement gods.

The first guy I called was your typical older, retired jack-of-all-trades, anxious to earn extra money.

"Hi, I'm Stacey," I gushed, opening the front door. "You won't believe how glad I am to see you." *Hallelujah!*

"What's the problem?" he said, all business. We discussed the most critical project on the list—the replacement of broken and missing bathroom tiles. After the discussion, I hired him. The job lasted more than two weeks. He showed up daily, grinding and drilling to completion.

"Thank you so much. You're the best," I said, laying on compliments as thick as pea soup.

A good man is hard to find.

By week three, he offered a helping hand with a series of minor projects. He hung pictures, fixed a leaky sink, and cleaned out the garage. I called him at home the next week to help set up Christmas decorations and lights—the works.

But his attitude changed by week six. I had a sneaky feeling he was cheating on me. He turned up late for our next appointment. And he started taking calls on his cell phone during work.

"Yeah sure, I'll be over in fifteen," he said, whispering into the phone now cupped in his hand.

What's this? Where's he think he's going? Who's he talking to? I brooded.

With nary an explanation, he hiked up his tool belt, grabbed his toolbox and skedaddled. I waited a few days before I called him again.

"This is Joe. Leave a message," said his voicemail.

"Joe, please call me. I need you for several small projects. I could really use your help. Thanks."

Weeks passed. Finally he dropped by to collect his last check. "By the way, I'm raising my rates and I'll be tied up a few months with a big job."

And just like that, my handyman dumped me.

After Joe, I found Rusty through his online website, RustyDoesJobs.com. Based on his profile pic, he didn't look like a mass murderer. Best yet, he could start the next day.

He arrived fifteen minutes early. I answered the

door wearing ratty sweatpants and my old high school sweatshirt.

"Hi, I'm Rusty. You needed a handyman?" he said, looking me up and down.

Hey, Buddy. Take a picture, it lasts longer! I thought, not happy he arrived early for our date.

Once he put his eyes back in his head, he began the first job, hanging a ceiling fan in the den. From the top of the ladder, he asked, "How far do you want the fan to hang down?"

"I don't care," I said, tugging on my ear.

"Six inches or twelve inches?" he asked, with narrow, squinty eyes.

"Uh, I don't care." *Stop pressuring me.*

He settled on twelve inches. Then I proceeded to talk. I couldn't be stopped. I had no idea if he even answered me. "Did you watch the Giant's game?" "Can you believe the weather?" "How long have you been a handyman?" "My last handy guy never called me back. I think he's avoiding me."

"No kidding," he said, letting out a gasp.

When he finished replacing the fan, then repairing the toilet, he said to use PayPal to pay him, grabbed his things, and rushed out.

"Wait. Can I just mail you a check?"

"I don't use snail mail."

He's afraid to give me his address. "I guess this is good-bye?" I yelled after him, receiving no answer in return. *Another one bites the dust.*

Then my lucky day arrived. My realtor introduced me to José and the heavens split open. He had all the necessary qualities—loyalty, strength, and sensitivity. And he was hardworking. A match made in honey-do heaven.

Whatever the task, José proved to be an expert. And he listened and respected my opinion. "Tell me what you need," he said, leaning forward and giving me steady eye contact.

"I don't know how to store all this junk in the garage," I said.

"No worries. I'll build you shelves."

When his cell phone rang he said, "Lo siento. I'm with a customer. Call you later."

At the end of the day, he asked, "If you have a problem, I can come back Sunday."

"Wow, I really appreciate that." I smiled. "I'll be OK."

"Make your list then. See you Tuesday."

Yeah! He likes me! He really likes me! This was the beginning of a beautiful relationship.

SELF-CHECKOUT

Shopping at Safeway during rush hour can be as stressful as trying to program a DVR player. After selecting my grocery items, I stand in a lane five customers deep, filled with overloaded carts. I notice a few brave souls with small orders using self-checkout.

For those whose haven't been paying attention, the self-checkout is an automated register located near aisle one. The customer scans, bags, and pays for the purchases without the help of a cashier. Sounds easy enough, but don't let that fool you. Self-checkout machines can be cantankerous.

I eye the machine speculatively. "Don't do it. Remember the last time," says that little voice inside my head. I had selected Spanish instead of English and ended up in a system loop, "Llame al attendant." I abandoned the items on the scanner and left the store.

But today I have lots of motivation. I'm in a hurry and self-checkout offers salvation: faster and shorter lines. I refuse to be intimidated again.

I weave through other shoppers to reach self-checkout. One cashier provides assistance for six machines. With shrewd, beady eyes and painted-on pants, she acts like a periscope on a submarine, constantly scanning and waiting for the slightest customer infraction.

I step up to the self-checkout machine. A computer-animated voice demands that I follow the directions on the screen. First, I select English, not Spanish. Next, the robotic voice says, "Scan your item. Place in shopping bag." This goes smoothly until I try to scan a bag of carrots: no bar code.

Oh God, now what?

The attendant senses my confusion and saunters over. "Have a problem?" she asks.

"Yeah, how do I scan vegetables?"

She demonstrates, mocking me with the fluidity of the process. She places the carrots on the scale, enters a secret pin number, pushes four buttons, smirks, and walks away.

It is more difficult to repeat the steps without her by my side. Placing apples on the scale, I push the "No Bar-code" icon and then "A" on the display screen for apples. Forty separate icons appear. Mackintosh, Granny Smith, McIntosh, Red Delicious, the list drones on. Since the tiny label fell off the apple, I panic and push any button. My face turns beet red and my lips quiver.

Okay, just relax.

My items overflow the bagging area and I sling them into the cart. The register shuts down with an error message, "See attendant."

The computer system alerts the cashier. She marches over, fixes the machine, and reminds me, "You have to leave the bags in the bagging area until you're finished or the machine thinks you're stealing."

If I knew so much, I'd be working here.

By this point, crowds of impatient shoppers have

piled up behind me. Hyperventilating, I try my last item, a birthday card. I run it over the scanner and slide it into the bagging area.

The creepy computer voice reminds me, "Place item in bagging area."

What the hell?

I catch the attention of the attendant for the final time. She drags herself over, letting me know with the shake of her head that I am beyond help.

"The card is too lightweight. The machine doesn't know if you put it in the bagging area."

She enters another secret pin number, pushes a button, and walks away.

Finalizing my purchases, I scan my club card, enter the Visa, take the receipt, grab the last bag, and leave the store in humiliation. I didn't even dare attempt to use a coupon.

You've been warned.

TOILET PHOBIA

~~~~~~~~~~~~~~~~~~~

The thought of using a public toilet raises my anxiety to threat level orange. My fear started at Girl Scout camp in sixth grade, when I was accidentally locked in a ripe latrine during a Midwest heat wave. It was an experience that would have given anyone a case of toilet phobia.

During her senior year in high school, my daughter played on the varsity basketball team as center forward. The final game that season was held at the opponent's gym. For the first half, the two teams went back and forth. By the end of the second half, the girls were trouncing the cross-town rivals on their turf and the fans were as rowdy as a mosh pit during a hard rock concert.

But I was miserable. With only five minutes left of the game, I could not fight the urge to use the toilet any longer. I rushed from the gym, gasping as I banged open the women's restroom door. Thankfully it was a tiny bathroom, three stalls, all empty. Mindful to touch as little as possible, I did my business as quickly as possible.

Drying my hands on a paper towel, I turned toward the door. I yanked on the handle and then realized the janitor must have locked the door, since the game was almost over. I was trapped. Sweat broke out on my chest and armpits. My worst fears were realized. I was stuck in a bathroom with no way out and, of course, a cell phone out of juice.

Pressing my ear to the narrow crack in the steel door, I prayed for the sound of human voices on the other side. Hearing the crowd scream during the final moments of the game, I panicked and clawed at the door like a caged animal.

With a dry mouth, I yelled, "Help me. The door's locked. Anyone there?"

Nothing. Silent as a funeral. Mine.

A nervous twitch formed at the inner corner of my eye and worked downward to my neck. Irregular heartbeat. Spasms.

Trying to pull the door off its hinges, I leaned back on my heels and began shaking again. No luck. My eyes blinked with the speed of a strobe light.

But then I heard an angel, a low, melodious voice from the other side of the room, "Don't worry. I can help. You're okay."

Turning toward the voice, I witnessed a mother, eyebrows twisted with concern, clutching the hand of a small child. She looked familiar. How did this genie get into the bathroom? Then I spotted the other door. I had been trying to exit the door that backed to the boys' locker room.

My chest flushed bright crimson. "I am so embarrassed. Big hurry to get back to the game and tried to go out the wrong door."

"Don't worry about it," she said, running a hand through her hair. "Are you okay?"

"Fine now. Just mixed-up. Thanks."

I bolted the bathroom, passing a group of kids from the boys' locker room. They paused, foreheads wrinkled in confusion.

"Don't worry. That lady in there yelling? I helped her get out. She's fine now," I said.

A little white lie never hurt anyone.

HAIR TODAY, GONE TOMORROW

I know a few things about life: don't take candy from a stranger, do not stare at someone's boobs, never eat food off the floor, and you get only one chance to make a first impression.

While it might be too late for me to undo what happened after breaking some of these rules, maybe it's not too late for you to learn from my mistakes.

"Hey, we're getting together for drinks this weekend at our place," said my next-door neighbor, walking towards my car. "Bring a dish to share."

"Sounds good," I said. Sweat beaded on my forehead. Did she have any idea who she's asking? Cooking and I do not meet eye to eye.

I struggled to make a selection, scanning Grandma's cookbooks and Internet cooking sites. I called my mother-in-law for her insight.

"Got any ideas for an easy appetizer?" I asked.

"Sure, I'll email you a few recipes for party snacks. Best bet, try the stuffed mushroom caps."

The night before the gathering, I tested the spicy mushroom delights on my husband. "Try one and let me know what you think." Cheese and juice rolled down his chin. He smiled and said, "Me likie."

From then on I brought mushroom caps to every event I attended: holiday parties, fiftieth birthdays, bar mitzvahs, Sunday barbecues. Sometimes I added a pinch of cayenne pepper to amp up the hotness, or tried different cheeses like jalapeno or Parmigiano-Reggiano. Friends crowned me She-Who–Makes-Mushroom-Caps.

"We're having a get-together this weekend. Can you bring your mushroom caps?" everyone asked.

Sure thing.

Eileen, brand new to the subdivision, was hosting an open house on Saturday. "Bring your specialty," she asked.

My chance to make a memorable first impression!

This was going to be a particularly hairy weekend since I was also hosting a cookie exchange on Sunday. To save time, I decided to whip up a double batch of mushroom caps, one for the cookie exchange and another for the party.

Aluminum mixing bowls glistened on the counter. I dumped the necessary ingredients into the bowls: spicy sausage, breadcrumbs, mozzarella, and onion. Stirred like a madman. Swish, swish, swish went the bowls, glowing in the overhead fluorescent lighting.

Whap. The greasy metal bowl flew out of my hands and sailed across the kitchen. It landed upside down at the base of the refrigerator on my clean floor.

Oh crap!

Ingredients lay face down in a steaming pile. I hesitated for a second and then did the only thing I could do. I scooped up the portion nearest the top of the heap and plunked it back in another bowl. Ten-second rule.

I stuffed the reclaimed ingredients into the empty

mushroom caps, sprinkled with Parmesan, covered with Reynolds Wrap, and placed into the refrigerator.

That evening, I heated one portion of the appetizers for the party. At Eileen's, I set my pan in front and center. Pièce de résistance.

Partygoers snagged the hors d'oeuvres as fast as a kid in front of the dessert tray.

A smile spread across my face. I spied my husband in the crowd, a mushroom cap perched on a napkin in his hand.

"Come here," I said, flagging him with my hand. "What did you think of the mushroom caps? They're almost gone."

I watched as he took a big, juicy bite. Then he pulled the napkin back a few inches, crossed his eyes and yanked out a long blond hair from between his teeth.

"They're delicious, but I found a few hairs."

"WHAT???!" I said, hands trembling. "How many did you eat?"

"About five."

At that same moment, I spotted Eileen about five feet away. I watched in horror as she spit a mushroom cap into a napkin.

"We've got to get out of here," I said, bolting across the room, grabbing the half-empty pan of mushroom caps as I ran by.

Tray in one hand, I tossed my husband his coat and sprinted out the door and down the street. I was She-Who-Makes-Mushroom-Caps, never to be forgotten.

At home, I rushed the refrigerator, pulled out the other tray of appetizers, and held the caps under the kitchen light to confirm my suspicions. I stared at an uneven crop of hair, waving at irregular levels.

I will be run out of town on a rail.

For the next six months, I pleaded an illness or family emergency in order to refuse any invitation to a party. I couldn't hide forever, though, and knew I could never show up with mushroom caps again. So now I consider store-bought as good as homemade. Nothing beats a day-old pound cake.

This is between you and me.

Signed,

She-Who-Brings-Pound-Cake

BLOCK CAPTAIN

Calling the SWAT team on a neighbor just kind of happened in my quest to fight crime. I started the Neighborhood Watch program on our road after the sixth home robbery within two years. Bad guys entered locked and unlocked doors, open windows, and even a doggie door. They stole laptop computers, iPhones, CDs, and briefcases left in cars. It was time to take back our street.

I volunteered to be block captain. Like the gossips on *Desperate Housewives*, I made it a habit to watch vehicles coming and going in the neighborhood. One early afternoon, on a school day, I drove into my cul-de-sac and saw a suspicious car in front of my house.

Hot damn, Mama's got a job to do.

The occupants of the automobile engaged me in a staring contest. Then they looked over their shoulders, scanned the area, and parked the Ford Mustang on the other side of the road.

Ha, got your license plate!

I drove into my garage, pressed the remote, peeked through the window blinds, and analyzed the situation. Three tall guys about twenty years old ran out of their car and rushed into the alley between the houses. Poof. Gone.

I kept an eagle eye on the alley, but no one exited. I considered possible scenarios. Cleaning people? Nope, they weren't carrying any supplies. Relatives? Why would they sneak in the back? After five minutes I decided it was time to call the Pleasanton Police Department.

"I am the block captain for the Neighborhood Watch," I said, puffing up my chest to channel my authority. "I'm reporting a break-in at the Garfield Subdivision, corner of Pine and Main."

"Tell us what's going on," said the police dispatcher. I relayed the story with all the necessary details.

"Do you have the license number?" he said with a heavy sigh.

"Yes," I said, reciting six digits.

"You're missing a number. Can you get that for us?"

"No way. You told me to proceed with caution."

The cops arrived and set up a command center at the corner of our block, visible from inside my garage. The dispatcher told me to stay on the line and keep out of the officers' way. I remained vigilant and waited for action. A regular CSI California unveiled. Then four more guys arrived in full tactical gear, SWAT prominently displayed in white letters on black Kevlar vests.

Dear God, I hope it's not a cleaning crew inside.

Local officers and the SWAT team surrounded the front of the house wielding shotguns and circled the lot like a hula-hoop. They went into the backyard through the open gate between the houses and disappeared from view. My heart beat fast as I watched with anticipation. At the least, I expected shots or flares to explode any moment. After twenty minutes, from across the road, three tall men strutted out the front door, plopped into their vehicle, and zipped away.

Hey, what's happening?

Ten minutes later, I opened the garage door and peeked around the corner as the SWAT team escorted two teenage girls out the front door and into the police car at the corner. The gals were decked out: coiffed hair, short skirts, and high heels.

"The homeowners would like to thank you for calling the police," Officer Smiley said, walking toward me. "Their daughter skipped school. Had a party without the parents' permission. Invited college guys."

"Oh," I said, my eyes widened.

"Don't think they'll skip again. Good work," he said, verbally patting my head.

"Now what?" I said with nervous laughter.

"We're taking them back to school."

My teenagers pulled into our driveway as the police departed. "Hey, what happened?" my son asked. "Were the cops here?"

"Can you keep a secret?" I whispered. They nodded in unison and leaned in. "A gal down the street called the cops on the girl across the way," I said, glancing around to make sure no one heard me. "Looks like she tried to skip school."

"Oh brother," said my daughter, rolling her eyes as she strolled away. "Some people don't have anything better to do."

I'M GOING STRAIGHT TO HELL

I will hurdle pews to avoid shaking hands during church service. It's a germaphobe's nightmare.

Cold-and-flu season was at a peak. Public schools closed throughout the nation by the hundreds. People lined up at clinics for vaccines like they were giving away tickets to a Rolling Stones reunion tour.

"Maybe we should skip church today," I said to my husband. "You know, more people seem sicker than usual."

"I'm sure it will be fine," he said, grabbing our coats.

Yeah, right.

At church, even the pastor suffered a malady. "Good morning everyone," he coughed. With watery eyes, he continued, "Let's stand for a prayer."

Help me survive today.

I struggled to hear the service above all the hacking, sneezing, and throat clearing. Lozenges were passed around like jello shots. It was a veritable witch's brew of germs and I frantically searched for a way out before the sign of peace.

You know what I'm talking about. It's that moment before the scripture when the pastor announces, "Let us offer one another a sign of peace." Each parishioner extends his or her hand to the closest neighbor, usually within a four-foot radius.

But lately, it has gone well beyond reasonable limits. I have been at services where people practically hop over each other and jump into the aisle to say "Hi" or "Good morning." If offering the "Peace of Christ" takes longer that the actual service, it's time for someone to call "uncle."

But that's not my point.

To avoid contact, I will pretend to pick something off the floor right before the sign of peace. Or read the Bible, fall asleep, act engrossed in conversation, even fake a faint—whatever it takes.

During this service, I planned to bolt to the restroom. I mentally prepared my stealthy exit right after the children's service.

"Get ready to move over a bit so I can squeeze by you," I whispered to my husband.

"Where are you going?" he asked.

"You'll see."

I waited like a teenager for a text message. But today church was packed, stuffed like tamales in a jar. I ended up trapped, miles from the end of the pew.

And then the unthinkable happened. The parishioner in front of me had a coughing spasm more violent that a tsunami. Afterwards, he wiped his nose across the top of his hand and spit into a tissue. At that precise moment the pastor addressed the members, "Turn to your neighbor for the sign of peace."

I tried to claw my way past ten other people, but it was too late. The Cough turned around and snatched my hand faster than I could say "Holy moly!"

"Peace be with you," he murmured.

More like the kiss of death.

I stood paralyzed. My husband asked, "What's wrong? You look like you've seen a ghost."

Oh. My. God.

I remained frozen to my seat the rest of the service. As the pastor wished us farewell, we lined up to shake his hand. How can he do this each Sunday?

Like a politician, he grabbed my hand from behind my back and squeezed my sweaty palm. I walked like a robot to the car for a bottle of hand sanitizer.

What's wrong with trying a fist bump? Salute? Bow? Nod?

Next time I will be the one at the end of the pew wearing gloves and waving like the Queen of England. After all, she's ruled for sixty years and never shaken a single hand. This cannot be a coincidence.

DEATH, INSULTS, AND GEL MANICURES

My local nail salon is like a Turkish bazaar; people speak different languages, laugh, and yell surrounded by blaring music and bright lights. Nail polish bottles, Post-it notes, glossy posters, and banners with price lists of various nail services cover all available wall space.

Within moments of entering the salon, a man wearing a white mask rushed up and pushed me into the nearest vinyl chair. A tiny lady with a pink apron approached and said, "You want a mani-pedi?"

"Ummm...I want a gel manicure," I said, picking at a fingernail.

"Go pick a color," she said and thrust me towards an endless rack of polishes, ranging from pale yellow to fluorescent pink.

After I made my selection, she examined my nails and said, "When did you have last manicure?"

"Not since my wedding day."

"That figures," she said as she snipped away at my ragged cuticles.

She applied the polish as swiftly as my busy son finishes his homework. My hands glowed under fluorescent lights and dried in less than ten minutes.

"How long does a gel manicure last?" I asked the nail technician.

"Two weeks, maybe three," she said in a flat voice.

"Do I use nail polish remover to take it off?"

"You're a funny lady," she said with a smirk. "You come back to get polish off. We have special solution."

What? No one said anything about having to come back.

I stood up and reached for my purse to pay. She glanced down at my flip-flops and said, "You like a pedicure?"

"No, I'm in a hurry."

"How 'bout your eyebrows?" she said with an extended finger, pointing at my face. "Your husband will like you better."

I skedaddle out of there before they suggested Botox or a Brazilian wax.

At home, my husband noticed my long manicured nails. "Will you scratch my back?" he asked. "I heard gel manicures are bad for you, may even cause cancer."

A MAN'S HOME IS HIS DEATH-TRAP

I've moved eight times in twenty-two years of marriage. That's a grand total of 3,987 boxes to unpack, fifty pieces of battered furniture, forty-five missing cartons, fifteen damaged appliances, two wrecked cars, and one lost pet. I'm as unlucky as a cat in a room full of rocking chairs.

For our latest and hopefully final move, we found a perfect house only two miles away. This time our move would not be dictated by my husband's job. "Let's do this," I said to my husband after viewing the ideal home at an open house. "It's perfect."

Moving day swooped down on my household. "Oh. My. God. The movers will be here in ten minutes," I yelled, reaching for the alarm clock. "We overslept. Get the kids out of bed. Grab the overnight bag. Where's the dog?" I said, pulling my hands through my hair.

Two Strong Guys Moving Company stormed our residence and attacked with cardboard and packing materials. By noon, our place was wrapped in a shroud of paper and plastic.

Two days later a cleaning crew met me at the old house to prepare it for sale. I arrived early to insure things would be ready for the team. With my tote bag of cleaning supplies, I entered through the garage. In the dining room, I stared around in confusion.

"What's going on? Why are loose sheets of wallpaper all over the floor? Did someone break in and throw paper around?" I said to myself, stepping back and glancing up. Falling off the bulging ceiling was drywall—piles of wet, gummy white drywall.

Oh crap. The ceiling is going to explode!

I had seen the movie *The Money Pit*, in which a bathtub crashes down on someone's head in just such a scene. I leapt away and dialed the cell for help.

Mommy!

My trusty handyman rushed over to turn off the water main that had rusted shut. Next, I called my homeowner's insurance, a plumber, disaster recovery crew, and a general contractor to remedy the mess.

Final verdict: the movers had improperly unhooked the valves on the washing machine. For forty-eight hours, water from the laundry room had dripped down to the ceiling of the living room.

Thanks for doing a great job.

After two weeks, the ceiling was repaired. I met Dan, the general contractor, at our house to inspect his work. He emerged from a tomb of plastic sheeting covering the walls, ceiling, and light fixtures.

"Do you smell that?" he said, brushing off the fine powdered white dust from his shirt.

"Yeah, smells like burning wood."

"Kinda. Someone turned on the chandelier yesterday and forgot to turn it off. The plastic melted down over the fixture and the light bulbs. Man, you could have had a big fire."

Are you kidding me?

"Consider yourself lucky. Better buy some new bulbs," he said with a smile.

I'm soooooooo lucky.

MORE NAPKINS PLEASE

Did you ever notice that fast food places barely give you enough napkins to wipe off a pinkie after gorging on their messy fare? Seriously, it doesn't take an expert to know that napkins go hand in hand with sloppy food. Take my latest experience at a burger joint.

"Can I take your order, please?" droned a pimply teenage boy behind the counter.

After receiving my food, I spread out all its greasy goodness: burgers bulging with toppings, chili fries, drink, and condiments. What's that? One napkin. How can a diner survive with one napkin alone? Oozing, dripping bounty was a hallmark at In-N-Out Burgers.

I turned to catch a quick glimpse of my son. His approach to napkin scarcity was shared among the fourteen and under crowd. What's to complain about? Who needed napkins? As long as you are wearing clothes, just wipe the grease across your lips, down your face, and onto your sleeve! What's the problem?

Since I'm not comfortable using my arm as a napkin, I marched up to the counter and asked, "May I have a few more napkins?"

Totally serious, Pimple Face passed me one more.

Yeah, like that was going to make a dent. I'm talkin' lots more. A huge stack.

"Is it too much to ask for more napkins?" I barked.

That time, I swore, he went to a safe in the back of the kitchen and emerged with the prize napkins, doling two out like they were gold doubloons. I returned to the table with my prize. Since when did the guy behind the counter become the Napkin Police?

Now don't get me started about napkins at Subway, either. Eating lunch there had become a personal challenge. Inside the clear plastic bag were a tightly wrapped sandwich and one napkin. To clarify my anger, let me explain that I ordered a meatball sandwich. That sucker was so loaded with sauce and extras that just getting it to the table before it exploded was a challenge. Once unwrapped, the problem became urgent. Racing to the counter, I slipped my hand behind the cash register and stole five more napkins.

If it weren't for the fact that I could feed an army of kids for $5.99 at Taco Bell, I would probably stop going. That place definitely claimed a napkin shortage.

At the drive-thru window, I shouted, "Six soft tacos, one hard, nachos, small Coke. Don't forget the napkins."

Through the muffled intercom, the order sounded all garbled. At the drive-thru window I peeked inside my bag to find one measly napkin, one-ply, brown and dinky as a moist towelette. Come on. Mexican food was a messy meal, what with all the hot sauces and toppings. At the first speed bump, my lap will be one black bean away from looking like the Mexican appetizer platter. Rolling down the window, despite the line of cars backed up at the drive-thru, I demanded more napkins.

"Pull your car forward, lady," says Taco Guy.

"Not until I get more napkins," I said.

"You're causing a problem. Pull forward," he yelled.

"More napkins!" I demanded. He tossed napkins into my car amidst the sound of honking before I zoomed off.

One small step for mankind, more napkins for me.

IT'S A WONDERFUL KIOSK CHRISTMAS

On the sixth day of Christmas, the mall gave to me, six angry sales teams, five new languages, four aroma pillows, three tubs of sea salt, two hair straighteners, and a partridge in a pear tree.

As the refrain from "The Twelve Days of Christmas" echoes through my head, I wander the mall avoiding eye contact with kiosk employees. Who hasn't been stopped midstream by perky cell phone employees begging, "Try our service" or "Switch today"? Who hasn't had fragrant lotion squeezed onto their hands while taking cover from flying helicopters or tiny motorized cars zipping around their feet?

But while I try to avoid their seduction, the magnetic attraction is too strong.

Companies like Rosetta Stone consider Christmas to be the ideal time to learn Polish, Latin or Pashto, one of the two official languages of Afghanistan. Sure—with all my spare time when I'm not shopping, preparing perfect meals for an endless parade of relatives, or making the tenth batch of sugar cookies, no problem squeezing in some time to brush up on foreign languages.

As I hesitate near the kiosk, a snooty, suit-wearing

assistant manager asks, "Are you interested in learning a second language?" There are no high-pressure tactics here, but I can't help but feel incompetent listening to the long computer demo extolling its virtues. Walking away I hear, in the tiniest whisper, "your loss" spoken in English—or was it Arabic?

Wedged between Hollister and Express, Comfort Spa is poised for action, with workers slowly massaging their aromatic pillows, coaxing shoppers with lavender and mint scents. I notice the staff conferring among themselves as I approach, as they determine who will pounce first. Moments after making eye contact, an employee wraps me in a gentle hug of 100-percent all-natural hot scented products.

My next assaulter is tall and confident, striding up in a bold manner, massaging his pillow with large, fleshy fingers.

"Would you like to smell this?" he asks, pressing the soothing scents under my nose before I have a chance to answer. Within seconds, I look like the Stay Puft Marshmallow Man. What starts as a gigantic shoulder wrap progresses to a weird body belt encasing my torso in low heat. Next, he covers my face with a lavender eye mask.

"This next pillow has a very strong mint smell," Fat Fingers whispers. "Take a 'small' whiff."

Ignoring his warning, I suck in a huge whiff. My eyes tear and I get a brain-freeze-style head rush. After seducing me with his hot wraps, he calls in the big gun to complete the sale, the store manager. She catches my negative vibes and watery eyes. Realizing I'm a lost cause, she brushes me off. On to finish my shopping.

"Can I ask you a question?" asks Temani from Israel. Manning the Dead Sea kiosk, he attempts to form a close friendship, immediately confiding that he arrived in the United States yesterday and his English is a little rough. After rubbing Dead Sea salt into my hands and topping it off with a thick crust of lotion, he asks if I am ready to buy. For around $49.95, I could purchase the salt only. He stares in disbelief when I say, "This stuff hurts. If it's for dry, cracked skin, why is it so painful to rub in? I'm bleeding." His demeanor changes to irritation as I gaze hopefully at the nearby Starbucks.

I can't take the pressure. I need caffeine.

But not yet. Like a car wreck you can't look away from, I feel the pull of the next kiosk. I sample Herstyle, the hair straightening flat iron experts. At temperatures exceeding 400 degrees, this fashion accessory makes me a bit nervous but, throwing caution to the wind, I saunter up and willingly become their latest victim.

After "Natasha" straightens half of my head, I notice waves of smoke and a slight charred odor surrounding me. Sensing my panic, she says, "Don't worry. Your head smoking is normal." What a relief!

Alas, the kiosk is here to stay. I hope your self-discipline is better than mine. You've been warned.

Now if I can only find a way to make my hands stop bleeding.

BURNIN' LOVE

My love for a hot Sicilian started off innocently enough. But one thing led to another and a one-night stand became the beginning of a passionate affair. What started as sweet desire ended in extraordinary pain. I would be remiss if I didn't mention how this happened to a happily married, stay-at-home mom.

Pursuing my dream of becoming a newspaper columnist, I sought an opportunity to see my name in print and signed up to be a cookbook critic. Pizza cookbooks drew me into their pages, tantalizing me with cheesy delights.

Slinging pizza dough high in the air, Chef Emeril Lagasse had nothing over me. Homemade spicy marinara sauces simmered on the stovetop, crushed red pepper flakes and garlic kicked the heat up a notch. Whisking flour and pounding dough, my fists were as red and chapped as a deep-sea fisherman's.

Hot Jamaican jerk chicken pizza and zesty Italian sausage screamed, "Eat me!" Chipotle chicken with smoked jalapenos was a Tex-Mex delight. I became expert at grilling chilies over an open flame until the skin was black and blistered. Each pizza was spicier than the gossip surrounding the Kardashians.

My family delighted in the welcoming aromas emanating from the kitchen each night, tantalizing their nostrils and making their eyes water.

"What's for dinner?" asked the kids.

"Pizza again!"

"All right."

Overnight, salads became a distant memory. Scrumptious hot fare delighted my family and they demanded pizza thicker than a James Michener novel.

After two weeks of cheesy meals, I toppled over in pain, clutching my stomach. Falling into the nearest reclining chair, I begged for relief. Something was wrong: burning pain, spasms, cramps, and bloated stomach.

For years, I had watched my weight and the kids made fun of my fondness for salad. Zesty food? Not for me. How could I have anticipated that writing a cooking column would be hazardous to my health? The doctor asked, "Ever have your cholesterol tested? Eat spicy food? Cheese?" My initial response was an adamant "No."

Then I confessed my obsession to the doctor regarding the highly seasoned. Eating pizza had triggered a gallbladder attack. He told me I wouldn't survive the next cookbook unless I cut out the double cheese and fiery meat. And fast.

Not only that, he recommended I lay off alcohol, tomatoes, onions, fattening food, soda, red meat, dairy products, eggs, chocolate, and all things spicy. Even mints were on the list. A morning cup of Joe was scratched as well. But, on the plus side, artichokes, ginger root, coconuts, avocados, grapes, lemons, prunes, figs, currants, and low-fat cottage cheese were highly recommended.

I might starve.

Following the doctor's advice, my break-up with the bold and spicy needed to be as swift as an Olympiad running for the finish line. Despite my family's new cravings, we needed to move onto a spice-free diet or Mama would collapse.

Lunching at home alone, I picked my way through a mixed green salad with a thin slice of tomato topped with French dressing. Dumping the partly eaten meal into the trashcan, I spied a greasy box from Pizza Hut. "What's this?" I mumbled under my breath.

Their reaction to the new bland diet was to be expected. They had resorted to sneaking food into the house disguised in a generic grocery bag. After all, I had hooked them on yummy pizza then denied them what they craved. It was best to look the other way, my gallbladder be damned.

Let them eat cheese and spare me the guillotine!

HELL HATH NO FURY LIKE A WRITER SCORNED

Why can't I admit that I am a writer? If someone asks me what I do, I say, "I am a mother, CEO of the household, a teacher." But a writer? I learned that I couldn't deal with the unsolicited comments. Take last year's conversation with a neighbor.

"What do you do?" he asked one morning as he pulled his trashcan to the curb.

"Oh, I'm a writer," I said in my most serious tone.

"You know, when I retire I think I'm going to be a writer too."

"Yeah, when I retire, I going to be a heart surgeon," I mumbled under my breath as I walked away.

Telling someone you're a writer opens up an opportunity to be knocked down, criticized, and then asked stupid questions by complete strangers or nosey relatives.

"How much do you make?"

"That's a great hobby."

"Do you know J.K. Rowling?"

I'd been writing for years and realized that I needed a push to reach my full potential. "You should join the local writers' club to develop your skills," said my best friend. "And I heard there's a supportive critique group as well."

My fellow writers pushed me to submit a sample of my funny short stories to an online paper and presto: I had my own humor column. I developed an email list and sent out links to my bi-monthly column. Responses were supportive. Readers said, "I love your writing," or "You're so funny."

Then I opened an email from an old high school chum.

Oh boy, another compliment.

Wrong-O.

The email said, "You are a prolific writer. Congrats. Please remove me from your distribution list. Have a great day! Sarah."

I am a pain in the neck.

I returned for support to the one place that would appreciate my hard work, the writers' club. A story I wrote, "A Training Opportunity," was published in *Chicken Soup for the Soul: Magic of Mothers and Daughters*. I brought an extra copy of my book to the monthly meeting for the raffle and proudly placed it next to the rest of the donations. Mine was the only new title among used ones like *The Da Vinci Code* and *How to Fix Everything for Dummies*. Pulling a ticket from the hat, the vice president said, "Congrats, Jim. You get first pick."

With the smugness reserved for "those who have been published," I watched as he ambled up to the podium and made his selection. We were pals; he had cheered me on throughout my publishing experience. He reached over and grabbed...*War and Peace*?

Who the heck would take that one over my mine?

He sauntered back to his seat with a pleased smile.

The next raffle winner snagged *Webster's Dictionary*?

Oh, come on. We had lunch together yesterday. I thought you were my friend.

My paperback sat there as lonely as a comic book among the classics.

I am Wonder Woman.

Finally, a lady selected my book. A tear slid down my face.

After being published a second time, in *Not Your Mother's Book...On Being a Woman*, I was confident enough to hand out copies to colleagues and family. During a recent visit, my mother-in-law asked for a signed edition before we drove her to the airport.

"Here's a copy of my book," I said, handing it to her with both hands like fine china.

She snatched the anthology, stuffed it into her suitcase, and walked away.

Come back here. You skipped protocol. This is the moment you open the book, read the inscription, make a big fuss and tell me how terrific I am. You are doing it wrong!

I am a taxi driver.

Then the phone rang. "I just received your book in the mail," said my mom, breathless. "That's the best story you've ever written."

I'm Stacey Gustafson and I am a writer.

KEEP YOUR HANDS TO YOURSELF

A strange woman fondled my breasts, trapped me in an awkward position, and called me cruel names. For a while I tolerated her poor treatment.

I was getting a breast exam.

If you're like me, you postpone getting an annual mammogram for as long as possible. It hurts. But that little voice in your head keeps nagging, "Get it over with. It won't be so bad this time."

I entered Painfree Healthcare around the date of my annual physical. An assistant carrying a clipboard led me into the changing area and instructed me, "Strip to the waist. Put on this gown. Wait for the technician."

Moments later, a stocky lady with mousey brown hair strutted into the room and yelled, "Next."

That's me.

I followed her into the exam area and stared at all the equipment. A giant white box dominated the room with tubes and hoses dangling out like an octopus. Computers with jumbo screens circled the area.

I made a rookie mistake. "Welcome to the torture chamber," I said. The female technician hesitated, then stared me down.

"Oh, you're one of those?" she said, hands on hip. "Are you going to complain the whole time? Would you rather get cancer?"

Gee, that's a leap. Lighten up, Frances.

"You must have a low tolerance for pain," she said with a snap of her head.

That's it, woman. One more word and I'm gonna let it rip.

But I decided to wait until after my mammogram before saying a word. I worried the machine might "accidentally" break in the middle and leave me trapped in its pneumatic grip.

She pressed my body against the mammogram machine with her hands and then shoved my head to the right. "Now push your butt out," she demanded. "Bend your right knee. Suck in your stomach. Hold your breath."

Is that all? Want me to sing the Star Spangled Banner? Recite the alphabet backwards?

Then she proceeded to manhandle my breasts like a butcher on a side of beef. She squeezed, prodded and groped me into submission.

What? No small talk first?

"Now don't move," she said as she walked to the control panel.

Where would I go? If I fall, I'm going to have to buy some new bras.

The machine flattened my breast like a Swedish pancake. Due to the awkward position, I adjusted my weight to my other leg.

"This will be faster if you cooperate," she hissed in my ear.

When it ended, she tossed me my gown and with a

smirk said, "See how easy that was? Aren't you embarrassed you complained?"

I warned you.

"Lady, for your information, I have an unusually high tolerance for pain. I delivered two babies, ten pounds each, same as a pigmy hippopotamus. One without pain medication." *Take that.* "And I've had shoulder surgery, a gallbladder attack, and get my eyebrows waxed every two months." *Now who's the baby?*

I snatched my things and scooted out. And yes, I say it still hurts. Enough to skip a mammogram? Of course not.

NEW GIRL

"Is this piece of crap your idea?" asked Bob, one of the sales reps at Computers Plus, jabbing his finger into my face. "Are you the new girl?"

Hey, where's my "Hello, pleased to meet you" or "Welcome aboard," I wondered.

Before I started working at Computers Plus, I had the perfect entry-level job at a telephone company. Within three years, I doubled my salary and gained notice by the big guns on the top floor. The brass demanded my expertise for their largest and most complicated spreadsheets and integrated reports. The Go-to-Gal.

One hostile takeover later, goodbye dream job.

After a month's scramble, I cinched another entry-level position with a massive pay reduction at Computers Plus, a small computer company. Ralph, President and CEO, hired me to do sales reporting.

On my first day, Ralph discussed my most important task: preparation of reports to analyze sales figures for the year by territory. For my initial assignment, I collected data from the salesmen, like number of computer units sold and price. I used elaborate spreadsheets like the type I had created at the phone company. There I'd dealt with 2,599 sales reps. A measly twelve didn't offer much of a challenge.

"Are you the new girl?" Bob stamped his foot and stared me down.

Gulp. "Yes, I'm Stacey," I stammered, taking a colossal step back to dodge his spittle. "It's my second day."

"Great. Just great. I guess I'm expected to collect the data for all these reports?"

"Ralph asked me to gather the sales figures for the month from all the reps," I mumbled, looking down. According to my notes, the short, stocky guy in my face was Bob Shackleford, top rep; otherwise know as La Prima Donna.

"Well, tell him I have a family I never see and I'm not going to do his stupid report," he yelled, hands on hips. "Ralph can stick it!" said Bob, and with a final flourish stomped away in perfectly buffed wingtips.

What the hell was that? I've been hit by a dinky tornado.

After Bob's rant, I walked back to my cubicle and slumped in my chair. "Do I really need this?" I thought. "I can get yelled at anywhere. I'm practically working for free."

I shuffled through intra-office memos, gathered pads of paper from the filing room, sharpened pencils, and warmed up the computer. Then I heard, "Click-clack, click-clack."

He's back?

Bob, in his shiny tight suit and tiny loafers, headed straight for me. "Here, take your stupid report," he said, tossing it into my hands. I bent down to catch the last page. "Happy?"

This would not be my last run in with Bob Shackleford.

I kicked off each morning with coffee room gossip and a steaming cup of Joe, but as I rounded the corner, I detected the bark of an angry pit bull wrestling with a rawhide bone.

"Look at me. Just look at me," Bob roared and clutched the front of his pants with both hands. Covered with wet coffee stains, he ranted, "All I wanted was some stinkin' coffee. Some fool broke the coffee maker and it spilled all over the place."

"Do you need some help?" I asked, timidly backing away.

"New Girl, get me some paper towels." I stuffed four or five into his outstretched meaty palms and stormed the exit.

"Heard you got hit with Bob's rant," said the office manager at lunchtime. "You're doing a pretty good job handling his outbursts. Keep it up."

Easier said than done.

After two years, my husband announced that we were moving to Atlanta for his job. I submitted my two weeks' notice. Thank God.

For my final hurrah, I managed the FootJoy inventory: golf shoes and other apparel, like gloves, jackets, and socks. Sales reps handed these out like candy to customers as small tokens of appreciation. And the reps coveted a few for themselves.

As I restocked the merchandise on my last day, I detected the distinctive click-clack down the hallway. "Hey, New Girl, where's my HydroLite tan rain jacket?" Bob said, his nostrils flaring.

"Give me a second," I said, dropping my pen. "Got

to go to the backroom to find it." I rushed to collect his items and deposited them on his desk.

"Thanks, Stacey," he said. "Sorry to see you go. Take an extra jacket for your husband," he said. "No hard feelings, right?"

"It's been a pleasure."

ROOMMATE SURVIVAL GUIDE

Ever hate a person you've never even met? For me that was Joyce Ann.

My attempts to become a serious writer began in earnest three years ago, spurred by a dynamic guest speaker at my writers' club. She claimed opportunities for paid writing jobs were greater than ever on the Internet. She inspired me to submit my work to the local online newspaper, and they hired me as the weekly humor columnist.

I plowed through books like *The Complete Idiot's Guide to Publishing Magazine Articles* and *Comedy Writing Secrets* to perfect my craft—writing in the humor genre—and drafted a memoir. But I needed more in order to reach my goal of being a full-time professional writer.

Friends told me about The Erma Bombeck Writers' Conference, held every two years, with headliners like Phil Donahue, Lisa Scottoline, and Mary Lou Quinlan. I volunteered to work the conference and hand out flyers for a friend's new anthology. I would mingle with respected authors and gain connections in the publishing world. Maybe score an agent for my novel.

But the Marriott Hotel in Dayton, Ohio, was overbooked. Being stuck at a Holiday Inn, ten miles away, referred to by the attendees as the "Kids' Table," prevented me from reaching my goals.

Must worm my way into the Marriott, I thought to myself. Be closer to the action.

I struck gold when I received an email. "Hi, my name is Terri. My friend said you are looking for a roommate. Still interested?" she asked.

Hot damn, my lucky day.

"Sure," I emailed. "As long as you don't snore, grind your teeth, or have night frights, it's a deal." I canceled my original reservation at the Holiday Inn.

Fifteen minutes later, I received her follow-up email. "Hey Roomie, it's me. Forgot to mention one thing. Still trying to snag us two beds. See ya."

What?! One bed? This woman's a stranger. Wonder if I can get my room back at the Holiday Inn?

At check-in they confirmed my worst fear—one double bed.

"Uh, there must be some mistake," I said to the perky twelve-year-old attendant. My mind whirled with crafty ways to get out of this situation.

"Nope, says right here. One bed," she said with a snap of her gum.

"This won't work. I don't know my roommate. She broke out in a weird rash days ago, may be contagious and bleeding. Please, please check if there are any rooms with two beds left."

My scheme paid off, two beds. Take that, Marriott.

In the morning, Terri, my roommate, knocked on the door. A petite, spry woman, she described herself as "the oldest person at the workshop," seventy-five years young. She chatted nonstop with the unbridled enthusiasm and stamina of a sixteen-year-old girl.

I'm exhausted already.

"I guess you know the situation," she said. "My roommate was supposed to be Joyce Ann. Her husband got sick at the last minute. Had to cancel."

"That's too bad," I said, hiding my glee.

She rushed to the computer, click, click, click, then turned it my way. "Here's a picture of Joyce Ann. Isn't she beautiful? She's an actress, you know. Oh, I miss Joyce Ann."

I hate Joyce Ann.

"Yes, she's beautiful," I said, patting my hair into place.

"She was going to fix my hair real pretty and show me how to put on makeup." Then she did a quick once over on my face. "Maybe she could have helped you, too."

The first day of the conference ended after eight long hours of sessions such as "Chick Wit: Writing the Humorous Memoir" and "Editing for Bigger Laughs (Or Why I Wouldn't Want Two Vaginas)." I distributed hundreds of postcards announcing the call for submissions for my publisher-friend and collected business cards from each attendee I met.

Around midnight, with heavy legs and sore hands, I begged Terri to turn off the lights. If I was going to be a rich and famous author, I needed my zzzzz's. "I'm pooped. You going to bed soon?"

"Nah, I have hours of emails to catch up on. Wonder what Joyce Ann did today?"

Why isn't she tired? Next year I'm staying with someone in her forties with a couple of kids, a full-time job, and way less energy.

The next day included more writing advice and sessions like "How to Get Published Successfully" and "Evaluating Your Book Idea." My head spun with the possibilities. At a book-signing session, a famous author even asked me, "Are you working on a book?"

"Why...um...yes I am."

"Send me a copy and I'll forward it to my agent."

My big break had arrived.

That evening, I floated back to my room. Terri worked on the computer and glanced my way. "You looked bushed. Want to get some drinks?"

Holy crap, woman, you're bionic.

"Thanks anyway, but I have a shuttle pickup at 6:00 a.m.," I said and pulled the covers around my neck. "Better say our goodbyes now."

"I bet Joyce Ann would have stayed up all night and shared funny stories," she said. "Did I mention her lovely hair? She's in commercials."

"Geez, you're starting to hurt my feelings," I mumbled, squinting past the comforter. "Enough already about Joyce Ann." *Why don't you marry her?*

"Gosh, I didn't mean to get you upset," she said. "I bet Joyce Ann wouldn't have been so grumpy."

In the morning, I tiptoed out the door, dragging my overstuffed suitcase filled with postcards, notebooks, and eight author-signed books. Joyce Ann may have beauty, fame, and an uncanny ability to hypnotize senior citizens, but at the end of the day, I bagged an agent for a book deal and maintained my dignity.

Take that, Joyce Ann.

IT'S ALL RELATIVE UNTIL THEY DRIVE ME CRAZY

FANCY MEETING YOU HERE

Here's the thing you need to understand about my mother: she has short ash-blond hair, olive skin, pencil-thin eyebrows, and is just too friendly. Too talkative. Too neighborly. Too much. I am not sure if Pleasanton gets her.

Let me fill you in on a trip to Target.

"Can I help you find something?" my mom asked a complete stranger.

"Yeah, where are the dish towels?" she said.

"In aisle three. Want me to show you?"

"Do you work here?"

"No dear, just noticed you needed help."

You see what I mean? Now don't get me wrong, I love my mother. But seriously, sometimes her helpfulness can be exhausting. I'd have thought that weird looks from others and my red face would make her stop talking to strangers, but it only eggs her on.

At church, she goes way overboard greeting people. Last Sunday, I noticed a friend sitting a few rows ahead of us during the service. I nodded hello and thought that was that. But no. As we were lining up for communion, my mother nudged me out of the way, squeezed past five others, and practically laid her body across the row of parishioners to shake her hand.

"Hi, I'm Joan. Stacey's mom. From St. Louis."

Confusion twisted on my friend's face. After she recovered, she said, "Oh yeah, hi."

By the end of the service, my mother knew more church members than I did.

Afterwards, we strolled downtown for lunch and something sweet to eat. "Let's find a bakery," she said.

"Promise me you won't try to talk to everyone," I begged.

"Don't worry," she said with a smile and a shrug.

Yet despite my warnings, she amped it up like a kid on a sugar fix. At the bakery, she said, "Hi, my name is Joan. I'm from St. Louis. What's good today?"

The lady raised her eyebrows and rolled her eyes. She said, "Uh, how can I help you?"

"Those cupcakes look good. How much?"

"Four dollars. Each."

"That's kind of high. We'll take one."

Back on Main Street, she said, "That was weird. She couldn't care less if I ordered anything or not."

"I told you. People are too busy to talk. Pace yourself."

But lunching at the local deli was another story. The manager, cheery and vivacious, smiled as we reached the counter. Mom had found a kindred spirit.

"Hi, I'm visiting from St. Louis."

"That's great. What would you like to order?"

"Oh, it all sounds delicious. I'll take the Aunt Amelia's on Dutch crunch."

"Good choice."

The manager welcomed my mom and engaged her in conversation, asking about the weather in St. Louis and checking to see if she had a safe flight. But now I was getting annoyed.

"Come on Mom. I am sure she has other things to do. Go sit down."

"I like your mom. She's fun to talk to," said the manager.

For the next hour, we chatted and laughed over our sandwiches. I went to refill the drinks. "Be right back," I said. I returned in a couple of minutes, but my mother had left our table and was sitting with another mother and daughter combo. *Where had they come from?*

"Mom, here's your Coke," I said with a sigh as I handed her the drink.

"I want to introduce you to a few ladies I just met."

We shook hands and the older woman said, "Hi, my name is Kathy. I'm from St. Louis."

Of course you are!

SLEEPOVER GONE BAD

~~~~~~~~~~~~~~~~~

Nothing is more frustrating than going back to my child-hood home and discovering that no matter how much I've changed, everything there remains the same. Floor-boards creak. Front door squeaks. Kitchen sink leaks. And my mother is not bothered in the least by any of it.

Traveling to the Midwest this winter, after flight cancellations, delays, and three schedule changes, it was no different. When I arrived at my mother's front door, she grabbed me by the shoulders and smothered me with hugs and kisses. We talked for hours, but then I needed to break away and get rid of the airplane grime.

"I'm gonna take a fast shower," I told my mother.

"No problem," she smiled. "You know where every-thing is."

I flung back the shower curtain and the memories came flooding back. I remembered that the shower required specific instructions in order to operate. Okay, what's the deal with the knobs?

"Mom, how does this shower work again?" I asked, squinting to read the dials for on/off.

"Right faucet's hot, turn right. Left faucet's cold, turn left."

Back and forth I turned the knobs swifter than a disc jockey at a rave party. The shower boasted only two temperatures, either magma hot or liquid nitrogen cold. I stepped in one toe at a time, biting my bottom lip.

I twisted a lever at the top of the showerhead to start the flow. What began as a soft whine turned as shrill as a siren. Pipes shook within the drywall.

A shower for pygmies, not me at five-foot nine. Holding onto the wall with one arm, I leaned back to rinse the shampoo. Way back. And what's this? Lava soap? By the time I leave here, my face will be as dry and cracked as an inner-city sidewalk.

At bedtime, my mother suffocated me with two blankets and a comforter. Tucked in as tight as a straight-jacket, I begged, "Please don't turn the heat any higher. It seems just right."

"Fine."

No need for carbon dating: the mattress was left over from my elementary school days. To get comfortable, I curled into a fetal position and banged my knees on the wall. After twisting and turning, my head wedged between the headboard and mattress. I panicked.

"What's all that noise? Are you okay?" Mom called from her bedroom.

"No problem. Goodnight."

By 2:00 a.m. the heat in the house became unbearable. With a sharp intake of breath, I rose from my coffin with a massive headache, rushed down the hallway, and groped like a blind man for the thermostat. My mother had it set on "broil."

I woke the next morning to a fresh brewed pot of Kona coffee. Mom was excited to show me her wild birds.

"Take this black birdseed to refill the feeder. They love it. Why are you stooped over?"

Crippled from your mattress.

Those birds had been trained. Like a battalion of fighter jets, they ambushed me. Two woodpeckers, three yellow finches, and a cardinal had me in their radar lock as I raced to the bird feeder.

"Help!" I screamed, swatting birds from my hair.

"Oh, you big baby," she said, grabbing the birdseed out of my hand. "Just go inside, I'll feed them."

Birds swarmed my mother as I rushed inside for cover.

She's on her own. God help her.

Mom took every opportunity to introduce me to her friends. At the front door, I spied her talking to the mailman. "Mark, this is my daughter Stacey," she said, flagging me closer.

"Hi?" I said, patting down my hair to check for tangles and birdseed.

"Is she single?" I heard him mumble to my mother as I walked past them into the house.

The kitchen phone never stopped ringing my entire visit.

"Here," Mom shoved the receiver at me. "Talk to Virginia, she's waiting on the phone."

Ten minutes later, "Talk to my neighbor Susan. She just had a baby."

Then I tried to send an email using her computer, a device that displayed one character at a time. I typed half a page before the letter "T" appeared.

"Do you have a printer?"

"In the basement. Not hooked up," she said, shrugging her shoulders.

After six days and five nights, or 240 hours, or 14,400 minutes, I returned to Pleasanton. I was rewarded with dry, flakey, cracked skin, debilitating lower back pain, and a newfound fear of wild birds.

I may have outgrown my old bed and the Midwestern lifestyle, but despite all Mom's quirks, I love her more than ever. Her love is unconditional and she wants everyone to get to know me, so I'll put up with quirky house and gabby friends. Next time, I'll bring lots of hand cream.

RETURN TO SENDER

My grandparents' excuses for returning gifts ranged from too large, too tight, wrong color, useless, costly, confusing, or purchased under the wrong zodiac sign. Every present my mother or I gave them for the last forty years had been returned.

Apparently they had never heard that it was good etiquette to accept a gift graciously. "Return it, dear. We don't need it," Grandmother said in her girlish voice.

"Save your money. You keep it," growled Grandpa, tugging up his baggy trousers.

Each year, my mother continued to be disappointed and surprised by their insensitivity. "Mom, they do this every time," I said. "They hate everything we give them. Stop buying them stuff. Give gift certificates."

Instead, she took their rejection as a personal challenge. On my grandfather's birthday, she said, "I'll find something impossible to return."

She ordered a live, green potted plant from the local florist, from both of us. After the delivery, I called to ensure he had received it. I imagined he would say, "Thanks, I love it!" Alas, it was not to be.

Grandpa answered the phone and droned, "Thanks

for the silk arrangement." What did he mean by silk? We specifically ordered a generic, leafy houseplant. He described, with distaste, a basket full of red silk roses. Mom did not order this.

"Are you sure? Are you absolutely sure that it is silk?" I said. "Yep, red silk roses," he replied, then hung up. Plans to send even a simple plant backfired.

I immediately contacted the flower shop. After I described the problem, she said, "No way. We would never send silk. I have the order right here."

How could my grandpa confuse a silk floral arrangement with a potted plant? After a few calls back and forth, he continued to reconfirm, "Yes, it's fake."

"Are you sure there isn't any dirt in the pot?" I said. "Nope."

The florist picked up the arrangement at their apartment and scheduled another order to be delivered the next day.

With a told-you-so attitude, the florist called the next morning. "Your order came back to the store," she said. "Just as I thought, a ficus and Boston fern in a basket."

How could this be? Despite their age, their eyesight was perfect. They could spot a speck of lint on my blouse from across the room. What's going on here?

I shouldn't have been surprised that they weren't satisfied with the second order either. Brown leaves were the problem this time. They returned it in person to the florist and smoothly asked for the original plant back.

We were never certain about what really happened. In the future, I'm sticking to my original suggestion, gift certificates. It's impersonal and returnable, just the way they like it.

DON'T FORGET THE DUCT TAPE

Some of my fondest memories involve my father's ingenious approach to fixing things with duct tape. He used it to stretch the lifespan of shoes, pants, appliances, automobiles, toys, tools, and furniture. I remember when he customized his old slippers with duct tape, extending their lifespan another decade.

My father would often visit from out-of-town when the kids were toddlers to offer support when my husband traveled. Before my husband left, he warned, "Don't let your father fiddle with our stuff. He tries to fix it all with Super Glue and duct tape."

"Sure. I'll keep Dad away from trying to repair things," I reassured him.

But once my dad hit the front door my resolve crumbled. With young children it was difficult for my husband to squeeze out enough hours in the day to finish the honey-do list.

Dad said, "Can I help you by fixing anything this week?"

Can you ever! Say no more. Sorry, Honey.

He hung pictures, unclogged toilets, and painted a bedroom. "Anything else?" he asked.

"Well, our reception is really bad on the television. Think you can fix that?"

At that moment, like Jolly Ol' Saint Nick, his eyes sparkled and in a loud voice he said, "Where's the nearest Home Depot?" He returned with an antenna kit filled with current probes, cables, a tripod with azimuth and elevation head, Super Glue, and duct tape.

He climbed up the attic ladder dragging his supplies over his shoulder and disappeared for half a day. He shouted from above, "That should do it. Go turn on the TV to test it."

Later that weekend, my husband may have noticed the duct tape and glue but said nothing. At the end of the day, all that really mattered was the reception on the television was better than ever.

I SURVIVED THE PLAYGROUND

Nothing guaranteed a trip to the emergency room faster than being a kid in the '60s and '70s. Some say it was a simpler time for children: you could play outside until dark, catch fireflies, and ride a bike without a helmet. It was an era filled with unbridled fun. But I believe we're lucky if we survived the dangers that lurked in childhood.

Take our backyard play structure. After years of being left out in snow, hail, and rain, the swingset was a rusty contraption of frail aluminum with colorful, peeling paint. And my parents never dreamed of anchoring it into concrete. Its legs lifted two feet off the ground when we used the swings. A death trap in disguise. You needed a tetanus shot just to go near it.

Old-fashioned playground equipment, composed of nails, old tractor tires, heavy chains, and arsenic-laden paint promised skull fractures and lacerations. By comparison, today's play equipment is sissy stuff made of plastic, soft surfaces, well-maintained, and eco-conscious.

Driving by Veterans Plaza Park, crawling with kids, I reminisced with my own children, safely seat-belted in the back. Pointing out the window, I said, "During my time, if you weren't kicked in the head while you were playing, you weren't at recess."

Good times.

At home, I pulled out old family movies for my son and daughter. They hadn't heard of a glider and had no idea that it was yesterday's killing machine.

"What's a glider?" they asked.

"It's a swing with two benches that face each other. You pick up a lot of speed and could knock someone right off their feet if they weren't watching," I said, setting them on the sofa in front of the TV.

In the '60s, my dad had been one of the original owners of a Super 8 movie camera. He collected hours of my childhood: first steps, Easter egg hunts, and birthdays. But the moment I remembered the most I called, "Lucky to Be Alive." The scene began to run scratchy and fuzzy across the screen as I said, "Hey guys, here it comes."

Mesmerized, we stared at my three-year-old self walking across my grandmother's backyard picking daisies, inching close to the glider. My cousins were laughing and swinging with the enthusiasm of a circus act, rivers of dirt and sweat dripping down their faces. My dad, behind the camera, never stopped yelling, "Hey, Stacey, look this way. Smile."

After all those years, I gazed in awe. Back and forth like a scary pendulum, the glider nearly missed slicing off the top of my head. My father's laughter cackled on the tape. Why didn't he put the camera down to save me?

When the horror movie was over, my husband shared his own glider memory. "Yeah, that was nothin'.

Kids in my neighborhood used to dig a hole under it. Each of us took a turn underneath. You were lucky to get out before your mom called you home for dinner."

Like a game of Whack-a-Mole.

And did I mention the old-fashioned slide? Shiny metal, towering more than twelve feet high, it spiraled around and around, causing blisters, bruises, and concussions. Imagine August in the Midwest, 103-degree heat. Wearing shorts assured a third-degree burn. Sometimes we would add a little water to increase the speed, causing us to shoot down the barrel like a cannonball, landing with a splat on asphalt or concrete.

At the park near my house, the slides are not higher than six feet, a smooth-coated plastic surface with side rails, allowing children the luxury of a gentle descent with a cushioned landing. At the worst, kids today end up with a skinned knee on the play structure. Wimps.

Yesterday's play built character, made you tough—if you survived.

THE BIG SHOW

For thousands of years, man's best friend has been the dog. But what happens when dog's best friend is a cat?

Growing up in the Midwest, I tended to the usual menagerie of pets-gone-wrong—goldfish left in the sun, gerbils trapped in heating vents, and hamsters lost in the grass. I proved to be a complete failure at pet ownership, yet my parents rewarded me with a dog. Go figure.

One snowy night in December, a muffled *meow* emanated from our front porch. Mom cracked open the storm door, and a subzero blast of icy wind pushed her backward. She held the door open with her hip, glanced down and spied a tiny mixed tabby cat with faint brown and black stripes covering her body. The cat scratched at the door and tilted her head as if to say, "Please, may I come in?"

Our six-month-old mixed-breed puppy, Tippy, named for his black fur and white paws, released a high-pitched bark and turned in circles just inside the front door.

"Shhhh, be quiet," I said to Tippy, patting his head.

"Poor thing," said my mother, a sucker for homeless pets. "Must be freezing."

"If you let her in, she'll never leave," I said, with teenage authority.

By this time, Tippy had worked himself into a foaming frenzy and shoved his face through my mother's legs to get a better look at the cat outside.

Giving in, my mother opened the door a bit more. Wasting no time, that tabby cat strutted into the living room and pounced on our reclining chair. It commandeered a comfy place on the headrest and stared down at us, as if to say, "Now what are you going to do about it?"

"Why don't you make yourself at home?" I said to the cat.

From that moment on, Tippy and Ms. Kitty—her new name—napped together on the recliner, the cat balanced on the headrest and the dog curled up in a ball on the chair's cushion.

Those two became the best of friends. Whenever Tippy nudged Ms. Kitty with his nose and whipped his tail like a propeller, it signaled that playtime was on! They would tear out of the room, and Ms. Kitty would jump over Tippy's back. She would taunt him then skid under the bed, out of reach. Ms. Kitty was the one to decide when the fun was over by dive-bombing back to her spot on the chair.

The neighbors were aware of our pets' antics. Many times, they would holler from over the fence as they barbecued, "Bring out the dog and cat!" wanting a dinner show.

Let the games begin! And they did. Upon hearing their request, we would fling open the door, just like the parting of curtains at the Ringling Brothers Circus. The crowd cheered as Tippy pursued Ms. Kitty, the two dashing helter-skelter throughout the backyard. Next,

Ms. Kitty would roll into a ball and freeze in place, letting Tippy drag her around by the scruff of her neck. Then Tippy would toss Ms. Kitty like a baton across the lawn. Believe it or not, Ms. Kitty loved this and would race back to Tippy for a second act.

For the finale, Ms. Kitty would leapfrog over Tippy, just like famed gymnast Nadia Comaneci did in the Olympics. Back and forth Ms. Kitty flew, placing her front paws on Tippy's back as if he were a pommel horse. When Ms. Kitty did her amazing dismount, the crowd hollered, "Do it again! Do it again!"

A few months later, I noticed Ms. Kitty moving at a slower pace. She refused to budge from her perch on the recliner, even when Tippy did his best to egg her on.

"Mom, does she look a little fat?" I asked, bending closer to examine the cat.

"Yes. Ms. Kitty is soon to be a Missus," replied Mom.

One morning, Tippy howled at the top of the basement steps, begging us to follow him downstairs. Ms. Kitty was nestled in a cardboard box on top of the washing machine, surrounded by her four kittens, ranging in color from solid orange to striped gray. From that point forward, Tippy took up dog patrol at the base of the washing machine, overprotective of his pal and her kittens. If our friends leaned in too close, Tippy would let out a low growl—"Look, but don't touch."

After we found new owners for the kittens, Ms. Kitty disappeared. Tippy waited for her at the front door for weeks, but she never returned. Ms. Kitty left us the same way she came into our life, suddenly and with aplomb.

ONE MOM'S TRASH IS STILL CRAP

When it comes to emptying boxes after a move, I'm a regular whirlwind. I unpack and stuff everything into closets and drawers as swift as Apple develops a new iPhone. But during the last move, I regarded the boxes and thought to myself, "Why do I keep moving this junk around? What the hell is in these boxes anyway?"

I tackled the kitchen boxes first. As I unwrapped, it became clear that I have too much useless crap and made a pile called, "To Be Identified Later." That evening, I reexamined the heap and realized that all the items had one thing in common: they were gifts my mother had bestowed on me ever since my wedding day.

Congratulations! You've just won a new bagel slicer.

I scrutinized a piece on top of the mound. A six-inch silver metal utensil resembling giant tweezers. One end was pointy and the other end looked like a flat shovel. "Do you have any idea what this is?" I asked my husband.

"A salad bowl fork?" he said, glancing back at the newspaper.

Really? Maybe a back scratcher? Shoehorn? That doesn't even make sense.

"Then why is one end so sharp?" I asked.

"No idea. Ask your mom. She sent it."

In desperation I posted it on Facebook. Within fifteen minutes, I had twenty-seven friends willing to help me. Their ideas ranged from pizza cutter to olive splitter.

My friend suggested contacting *Cook's Illustrated* magazine to unlock the secret. The subject line of my email read, "Help! What the heck is this utensil?" Andrea Geary, Associate Editor, responded in less than an hour. "That's actually a vintage cookie scoop. You scoop your cookie dough onto the little platform and then squeeze the handle to deposit the lump of dough onto the cookie sheet. Clever, right?"

I definitely need this.

One thing I know for certain, a mother never runs out of hankies, advice, or impractical gifts. And my mother was no different. She visited me in California a few weeks after we unpacked from our move. Like a peregrine falcon, her eyes zoned in on the "To Be Identified Pile" in the corner of the kitchen counter.

"What's with all this junk?" she asked, picking up an item on the top.

"Stuff you've sent me over the years," I said, shaking my head.

"No way. Never seen it before," she said without emotion and moved away.

"Are you kidding? You sent this last month!" I gripped an object that resembled a life-sized hand with slender fingers, hot red nails, and a diamond wedding ring. Inside the palm of the hand was a circle the size of the bottom of a cup.

"Oh yeah, I remember. It's a cute cup holder."

More like creepy.

"And what about this?" I dangled a six-inch long by three-inch high white ceramic contraption with a central handle and five rings connected to a flat base.

"That's easy. It's a toast rack. Keeps the toast from getting soggy. Use it when company comes."

Should I host a black tie breakfast?

We poked through the pile one by one and discussed the pros and cons of keeping each. By the end, she convinced me that maybe I needed a fish-shaped platter to serve seafood and silver-plated iced teaspoons with crystal teapots at the tips for lemonade or iced coffee.

Mom knows best.

For lunch, we noshed on tuna salad sandwiches, veggies, and barbecue chips. I clasped a sandwich between silver-etched tongs with flat circular ends. As I dropped the sandwich onto her paper plate she stared at it with a dreamy expression.

"I love this," she said, grabbing it from me to hold in the light for closer inspection. "Where'd you get it?"

Take a guess.

FREE IS NOT WORTH IT

I shuffled through piles of paper in our junk drawer, chatting with my mother-in-law during her last visit. The conversation was innocuous enough until I deep-sixed stacks of coupons. Stunned, she jumped up and saved them from the recycling bin.

Woman, keep your hands out of my trash.

"Don't worry. It's just a bunch of free coupons, not worth it," I said, wiggling my head in disbelief.

"I have never found that to be the case," she said, hands on hips. "Free is free."

Not in my book.

Last summer, my friend's family was visiting and she expressed her concerns to me. "I don't know what to do. My mother hates going out to eat," said Sue. "She thinks restaurants are full of germs. But with three kids, I can't find the time to cook."

"Here, take this coupon. Buy one, get one free. The restaurant got a good rating on Yelp. Maybe this will change her mind," I said, forcing it on her.

The next evening, I stood on my driveway talking to my neighbor, Ed, when I spotted Sue helping her mother into the car. She had two black eyes and a broken arm.

I stared and shook my head.

"What the hell happened?" I asked, rushing across the street to get a closer look.

"My mom got a bad case of food poisoning, fainted over the bathtub, and used her arm to break the fall. We're on our way to the airport," she said, using the lady's good arm to guide her into the car.

After they zoomed away, Ed chimed in, "You think that's bad. Remember that carwash that opened last month? They went around hawking free services. Wonder why?"

"Yeah, I thought that was a nice idea."

"Nice? I sat inside watching as my car jumped off the tracks and was dragged the rest of the way, scraping the walls. By the final drying, it was missing the front bumper and rear panel. Free? Ha!"

I knew better than to accept anything free. I'd been warned. But some offers are too tempting pass up. The previous owners of our house wanted us to have a few items, if interested.

Are you talking free?

We were delighted to accept their old patio table. *What the heck?* Then we accepted a few rose planters. *Why not?* When it came time to snag their used washing machine and dryer, *heck yeah!*

Anxious to start the laundry during our move-in, I selected the permanent-press cycle, pressed go and went back to unpack.

An hour later, I checked the laundry. *What's going on here?* The tub was filled to the top with water. I tried to redo the spin cycle, reload the laundry and unloaded the towels. Nothing worked.

I called HandyGuys.com. Help was on the way.

"Can you fix this thing?" I pleaded with him.

He yanked out the wet towels and bailed forty gallons of water. After emptying the machine, he unhooked it from the wall and began tinkering with its insides.

An hour and half later, it was declared unrepairable and removed from the premises. A $50 disposal fee, plus $140 for the work. *Thank you very much for the free washing machine!*

Next time someone has something free to offer, like a coupon, remind me to call my mother-in-law. Pay it forward.

MAN OVERBOARD

Here's something I know: all you needed for date night in college was five dollars, someone's borrowed car, and any activity offered free of charge.

A friend called with a proposal that fit the criteria perfectly. "You interested in going to Lake of the Ozarks this weekend? Bring your boyfriend," said Scott. "You know anyone with a boat?"

"I'll ask around," I said.

The next day my father called to check up on me. "Any plans for the weekend?" he asked.

I knew my father would never let me use his boat but tried to drop a big hint anyway. "We're heading down to the Lake. It'll be a great time, but no one has a boat we can use."

"I do."

Yippee!

"Can we borrow it?" I asked.

"Sure, I'll even drive it down for you."

Gasp.

My father had wormed his way into my plans. Again. This was like the time he showed up unannounced at senior grad night. Or "happened" to be at the same restaurant where I had my first date in high school.

But I digress.

Early the next morning, Mike and I met my father at the local gas station to grab a few supplies, like Cheetos, Doritos, grapes, and bottled water. After two hours, halfway to our destination, Dad's car started shaking as violently as a washing machine full of wet blankets. He pulled over to the side of the road, hopped out, grabbed a toolbox, and yelled through the car window, "No worries. A flat. Just take a minute."

Is it too late to bail?

Bing, bam, boom, he fixed it in a jiffy and we were back on the road, speeding to make up lost time.

Rumble, chug, burp.

Oh crap. What now?

With a puff of smoke, the trailer tire blew. Like white lightning, Dad snatched a roll of electric tape, a tire pump, and Krazy Glue. A master of his craft. In thirty minutes we were back on the road.

Hurray?

Six hours, twelve bottles of water, and two tires later, we arrived at the cabin. My friends greeted us with cheers and offers of cold Budweiser. They patted my dad on the back, the man of the hour, the Boat Guy.

We barbecued burgers and consumed coolers of alcohol. Dad relaxed as my friends served him a constant stream of salty snacks and cold beverages. Within an hour, he snoozed on the sofa, a smile plastered on his face.

Dear God, I know that look. He's here for the long haul.

By day two, the ski boat bit the dust. Engine failure. Not a repair shop closer than a three-hour drive. "You guys all right with me staying?" Dad asked, bouncing on his toes.

"Sure Mr. L, no problem," said Scott.

Ugh.

For the rest of the weekend, we couldn't shake him. He was everywhere, cramping our style. On a quiet walk, he jogged alongside, "Hey, what a great day. Let's race." A quick trip to the mini mart, "Mind if I come along?"

"I'm so sorry," I whispered in my boyfriend's ear. "Please don't be mad."

Next morning, we took out the canoe and paddled to the other side of the lake. Alone time, no Dad in sight. Maybe we could sneak in a make-out session.

"I'm so sorry how this weekend turned out," I said, flipping my hair over my shoulder and batting my eyes.

"Don't worry about it," he said. "We'll have another chance in the summer. It's not your fault."

Then the silence of the morning was interrupted by a faint sound in the distance. Purr, whirl, purr. Buzz. Buzz. From the shore, about 100 yards away, someone waved.

What the hell? Who's that?

But I knew. He had found us, the human GPS. Like MacGyver, he had assembled a plywood platform and a small trawling motor on top of an innertube. He grew closer.

"Hey guys. I've been looking everywhere for you."

Three years later the understanding boyfriend became my husband. We moved 2,897 miles away. Boat Guy lives around the corner.

KING OF THE PYROTECHNICS

Juvenile delinquents and misfits gathered on our front porch on the Fourth of July, waiting for their Master of Ceremonies, the King of the Pyrotechnics: my father. An hour before dusk, the time when the mosquitoes rose out of damp lawns, he arrived home from a roadside fireworks stand, bearing bulging bags of explosives, legal and otherwise. As the crowd cheered, he poured the merchandise onto the driveway.

"Can I have some?" said a scraggly pre-teen boy, hands trembling, excited to be part of the danger.

"What does that one do?" said a young girl.

"Can I help you light them?" I said.

The pregame show began with entry-level fireworks like worms, sparklers, smoke bombs, and fountains. He passed around lit punks for each kid. They grabbed from the glittery pile and picked a spot to light the fireworks on the crowded, tiny block. This activity lasted until an hour after dusk. Black, smoking marks circled the area around our house. Police officers cruised the street, giving us the thumbs-up sign. In the '80s, cops were prone to look the other way.

My mother rubbernecked from twenty-five yards

away on the front porch, a cocoon of safety. "Be careful," she called, tapping her toes. "Stand back."

But her complaints fell on deaf ears. It was my dad's day to shine.

In front of our house, camouflaged behind thick clouds of smoke and the smell of sulfur and Off! Deep Woods bug spray, my dad prepared to light and distribute the real fireworks—Roman candles and spinners. The aerial part of the show had begun.

Explosives with names like Big 'n Bad, Absolute Pyro, Burn Baby Burn and Infantry ignited the sky with a pop, bang, whistle. A kaleidoscope of red, orange, yellow, green, purple, and silver exploded overhead and pieces of pasteboard tubes fell on us like rain.

For the late, late night portion he mobilized an army of adolescents for battle. Handcrafted three-foot metal pipes were distributed with loaded Roman candles. "Grab a partner and let's fire these at the kids up the street," he said. "One of you lights the wick, the other aims." The street sparkled with bright orange and white stars until one team surrendered or their mom called them inside for the night.

After we trounced the "kids up the street," we awaited the grand finale. And that year, Dad did not disappoint. For the pièce de résistance, he would blow the heavy iron lid off the manhole with two M80s, each having a quarter the power of a stick of dynamite.

"Hey you, Big Boys," he said to Mark and Scott. "Come here and help me remove this lid."

The rest of the kids watched from ten feet away as the Master carted off the lid with the aid of the miscreants. Once removed, he attached a fuse to the M80s and snaked it to down the sewer. Big Boys helped push the lid back into position as my father set fire to the fuse and raced to safety.

Kapow! We stared, stupefied, as the lid flew into the air and landed nearby.

Twenty years later, I know about the dangers of fireworks: property damage, third-degree burns, and fires. I would never dream of letting my two kids get any closer to fireworks than the front seat of our car or a beach blanket at a professionally managed display.

But forty years ago, for a brief moment, the Fourth of July was magical, a night to remember. And for a few hours, my father was the reigning king, a man who believed in the philosophy, "Go big or go home."

LETTER FROM MOM

Happy Thanksgiving! By now, you are probably waking from a deep slumber, wiping the crust from your eyes as you stumble into the kitchen in search of coffee. I bet it's about 10:00 a.m. and you're starting to wonder, "Where's Mom?" Well, surprise! I'm at the movies. I have decided to take the day off.

I'm exhausted by the thought of another Thanksgiving Day spent in the scullery, sweating it out like Bikram Yoga. Enough already with hot ovens, boiling pots, and disgusting turkey giblets. I'm Getting My Movie On, sitting in a comfy chair, hogging a whole box of popcorn and a large Diet Coke. Ha ha!

Now don't get me wrong, I love each and every member of my family, including the various friends and relatives staying the night. But I decided to take it upon myself to make this day more than a work-from-home day. I deserve time off, same as the rest of you, a chance to relax near the warm fireplace, watch television, maybe read *People* magazine.

Have you considered divvying up the work this year? I'll accept all offers to share in the responsibilities. Feel free to do the grocery shopping. Or maybe you could prepare the sausage stuffing, mash the sweet potatoes, or baste the turkey. Do something, for God's sake. And do not mention dietary restrictions. If you need low-calorie, vegetarian, gluten-free, or vegan meals, skip this holiday.

I'm sick of washing stacks of dishes as you fall into a turkey coma, saliva dripping from your slackened mouths. Was that last slice of cranberry crumble pie too much? Next time take a breather between bites.

Text me when you come up with a plan to relieve me from another weary holiday spent in the kitchen as the rest of you whoop it up in the living room, cheering for your favorite NFL team or laughing at the commercials. For twenty-two years, I've watched from a distance and never known the final score of the football game.

I'll be waiting to hear from you in the theatre. But you better hurry. The next movie caught my eye; Vince Vaughn is hilarious.

Love,
One Tired Mama

EAT, DRINK, EPIPEN

Sidetracked by a phone call, I had grabbed the wrong pill bottle. My eyes blinked faster than a strobe light when I realized I had swallowed my son's acne meds, not my One-A-Day Women's multivitamin.

I wasn't always so absent-minded. In my twenties, I could write Fortran code, answer the telephone, and build Excel spreadsheets—while driving to work. In my thirties, I juggled household chores, my husband's travel schedule, and two infants under three. After forty, I sharpened my sleuth skills by keeping abreast of teenage shenanigans. But as I neared my fifties, I developed complete and inescapable memory loss.

What's going on here?

Last week I whipped up my husband's favorite dishes, herb-crusted filet mignon, twice-baked potatoes, and green leafy Italian salad. I called him on his cell and asked, "What time will you be home for dinner? I made all of your favorites." Male laughter exploded out of the speaker phone. "What's going on?" I asked.

"I'm in Florida," he said. "Driving with a couple of guys to our next meeting. Won't be home until tomorrow."

Damn, I thought. He made a big deal about writing his trip on the calendar with a red marker. He circled the date, looked me straight in the eye and said, "Now you won't forget."

Wrong-O.

But nothing compared to the brain fart I experienced on the day of a dinner party. Before I left to get rations, I called my friend to firm up plans for the evening. "You guys still coming to dinner at six? Any allergies?"

"We'll be there. Don't forget, Frank's a pescetarian."

Come again?

"He eats fish but no meat," she explained. "And he doesn't do well with peppers."

In other words, he's a pain in the butt.

"No problem."

I prepared a detailed grocery list and skedaddled. As I loaded vegetables into the cart, I realized I'd left my precious list on the counter. *Relax.* "Just start with the basics," I thought to myself. I snapped up skim milk, a dozen eggs, and greens as quick as a shopper at a clearance sale at Barney's.

What am I making for dinner? Special requests? Think!

I had studied recipes for days to create the perfect menu. *What the heck was I making?* "Oh yeah! " I mumbled under my breath. *Steak, vegetables, salad.* My husband's favorite.

Ninety minutes until show time.

At home, I rushed upstairs to shower then plunged back downstairs to the kitchen. Cookbooks scattered about the counter, I ran my finger down an open page. Time to start twice-baked potatoes.

Potatoes? Where are the potatoes?

"Guys, do you know what happened to the groceries?" I hollered to my kids in a trance in front of the television.

"What are you talking about? We didn't see any groceries," my son said, turning back to *Duck Dynasty*.

"Did you bring the bags inside?" my daughter asked without taking her eyes away from the screen.

"Of course."

Shit!

I opened the door and stared into the garage. Abandoned bags dripped their contents on the hot garage floor. I hauled them up the steps.

"Oh. My. God. Where's the rest?" I asked myself. "I'm missing the steak."

In my rush, I had dumped a bag into the recyclables bin.

I'm really losing it.

Thirty minutes until show time. *Remember, Frank's a picky eater*. Check. *Avoid green peppers*. Check. I stuffed the steak into the broiler as the doorbell rang. Frank and Mary arrived right on schedule. My husband blew in through the garage door.

"Here, let me take that," I said, reaching for Mary's jacket. "Glad to see you. Come on in."

Grilled beef with a mix of garlic and herbs filled the air.

"Smells delicious," Mary said. "What are we having?"

"Red wine, steak, and twice-baked potatoes."

"Frank doesn't eat meat," she said walking into the dining room. "Remember, he's a pescetarian."

"Um, I thought you said he was persnickety," I said, frowning. "I made salad."

As we dined on steak, Frank devoured his salad.

"This is delicious," he said staring into a wooden salad bowl.

"Thanks," I beamed. "It's my signature salad." Frank's face turned red and he scratched his arms and neck. "Are you OK?" I asked.

"Man, I feel funny," he said. "Are peppers in the salad?"

"Nope," I reassured him. "Romaine lettuce, parmesan cheese, artichokes, olive oil, and pimentos."

"He's having an allergic reaction," said Mary, clutching Frank. "Pimentos are peppers."

I'm an idiot.

They dashed for the door as Mary searched for the EpiPen in her overstuffed Coach purse.

"I'm sorry," I mumbled, shoulders hunched.

After ten minutes, my cell phone buzzed. Mary texted, "False alarm. Frank's OK. A little Benadryl did the trick."

That was close.

I stuffed my phone in my back pocket and I felt a crumpled wad. "Get fish. No peppers."

FOR YOUR EYES ONLY

I'm going blind. Sure, I can still see far-away objects with contacts, like a traffic light or a mother pushing her baby across the street in a stroller. And I have magnifying vision from about one-eighth of an inch away, like a superhero, but that rarely comes in handy. Yet in the distance from the end of my nose to twelve inches away, I've got nothin'.

Around forty-five, my near vision started to disappear as slowly as a teenager washing dishes. I first noticed I needed reading glasses when I was enjoying *The Housewife Assassin's Handbook*. In my dimly lit bedroom around midnight, snuggled into a down comforter, I stared at the page, tried to focus, and blinked. Blink. Blink, blink. In one instant the page was clear and the next, WHAM, I couldn't see a word. I turned the book at a thirty-degree angle, bending and twisting the pages. Still blurry.

I leaned over and nudged my husband, "Can you read this?"

"Of course. No problem." *Mr. Perfect Eyes.*

"Seriously?"

"Yeah."

The next day, I hightailed over to Cross Eyes Optometric Group for my annual exam. He challenged me with a laminated notecard, teeny writing.

"Read the last line," he said, settling back into his chair.

"You're kidding?" No one could read that! It looked like specks of pepper sprinkled in a straight line.

"If you can't read the last line, try the first line, please," he said as he moved the card at arm's length.

I squinted, "Is the first letter 'A'?"

I left the office with two pairs of reading glasses. Nine months later, I worked my way up to three stronger prescriptions, +1.25, +1.50, and +1.75. At that rate, I would be using a white cane in time for Fat Tuesday.

As I dressed for lunch with friends, I peered into the mirror and spied two black dots for eyes staring back at me. After five tries at applying mascara without readers, I jabbed the wand into my eye. Black watery streaks ran down my face. I dabbed the mess with a tissue and opted to remove my contacts and wear glasses instead.

Minus one eye, I tweezed my brows. Like reading braille, I ran my fingers across the hairs, struggling to find any strays. In a flash, I lost an eyebrow. *Must repair with a pencil. Maybe no one will notice*, I thought.

Down one eye and an eyebrow, I figured the rest would be a cakewalk. Wrong. Remember when you wondered how the heck grandma could get the lipstick on her teeth and miss the lip line by a mile? Now I know.

I caught my reflection on the way out the door. The Picasso portrait that stared back horrified me. Since I was running late, it would have to do.

At Athens Grille and Wine Lounge, I greeted everyone with a hug.

"Oh, I see you're wearing glasses," my friend said, tilting her head.

"Poked my eye with the mascara wand. No biggie."

With only prescription lenses for distance, I struggled to read the menu.

"Does anyone have a pair of readers I can borrow? Left them at home," I said, rubbing the back of my neck.

Three pairs of hands started digging into ginormous purses but came up empty. Panic. Not one of us could see well enough to order. We scanned fellow diners for a pair to borrow.

"Can we borrow your glasses?" I asked an elderly lady at the next table who was wearing reading glasses on a chain around her neck.

We passed her readers around the table. When the waiter returned to take our order, I hurriedly stacked the readers on top of the prescription frames. His forehead scrunched up and his eyes wandered around my face. *Take a picture, it lasts longer, Buddy!* I was so frustrated that when he asked for my order, I pointed at the salad on the menu.

Fifteen minutes later he returned with eggplant borani. "Lady, that's what you pointed at. Want something else instead?"

"Whatever."

Despite being aggravated by my vision loss, I tried to focus on the conversation. After an hour of chitchat about husbands and kids, we gathered our purses and paid the bill.

"Let's split it four ways," I said. "It's my turn to leave the tip."

I dropped a two-dollar bill on the table. Looks a lot like a twenty.

IS THERE LIFE AFTER ORTHOTICS?

In my forties, I could finally afford to purchase the expensive footwear I had always envied: classic Dior black pumps, Coach tennis shoes, and jeweled strappy sandals. But nowadays, comfort overrules my desire to be a fashion plate, and low-heeled pumps, white sneakers, and flats get me from church to the gym.

Recently, when it was time to replace my favorite footwear, I called on Sandra, my shopping buddy. "Wanna go to the mall?"

"Sure," she said. "See you in fifteen."

Sandra waved me over as I entered Mega Mall and grabbed me in an embrace. Staring down at my worn-out tennis shoes with scuffed soles and frayed laces, she said, "Finally decided to break down and invest in some new shoes?"

"Yep, it's time," I said, marching over to the displays. Squeak, squish. Squeak, squish.

'What's that noise?" she said, twisting her head around.

Is she talking to me?

Taking a step back, she asked, "Are you wearing orthotics?"

"Oh my God," I said, covering my face with my hands. "I got so used to hearing it, I didn't notice."

"Try adding baby powder under the soles. Cuts down on the sound."

I'm a forty-seven year old woman with eighty-year-old feet. What happened?

I remembered that in my twenties, I craved a closet stuffed with sexy high heels, jellies, Candies and espadrilles. To hell with comfort and arch support. I cared only about the latest trends and affordability. I put up with uncomfortable shoes as long as they were in style, even wore the wrong size.

My recent visit to the orthopedic specialist for painful arches was a testament to my foolish lack of concern for proper foot care. The podiatrist confirmed what I suspected. The natural aging process plus a lifetime of wearing cheap, ill-fitting shoes had forced me into orthotics. Dr. Tootsie cast my foot in plaster and in three weeks called me back to test-drive the custom-molded shoe inserts, guaranteed to relieve foot pain.

"Pull out your old soles and replace them with these," she demanded, glaring down at me from her stool. *Ms. High-and-Mighty.* "Now walk the hallway and I'll watch your stride."

Yowza.

Up and down I strolled. Squeak, squish. What a glorious feeling. Screech, squawk. I floated on a fabulous cushion of air. Squish, squawk.

What the hell's that racket?

"Um, these feel great but why are they so loud?" I asked, scrunching my eyebrows together.

"Don't worry about it," she reassured. "They need time to break in."

And then I forgot about it and got used to the noise.

Sandra jolted me out of my trance with a tap on my shoulder. Staring at the rows of shoes, I realized that in addition to orthotics, I'd downscaled to Hush Puppies and Easy Spirit. *Ah, the sad reality of getting older.*

An awkward teenage sales clerk wandered nearby, half-heartedly straightening shoes on display. "Can I help you, lady?" Shoe Guy mumbled, studying my feet.

Hey Buddy, eyes up here.

"I need comfortable, supportive tennis shoes," I said, settling into a chair. "Show me all you've got."

As the bushy-haired sales guy searched for my selection, Sandra handed me a pair of taupe suede TOMS. "What do you think of these?" she asked.

"Not in a million years," I said, shaking my head. "Those soles are a piece of cardboard."

After ten minutes of rooting, Shoe Guy returned with an armful of boxes with names like Total Motion, Grannies Best and Ortho Feet. *Soon I'll be wearing house slippers with cutouts for my corns and bunions,* I thought to myself.

Hasta la vista, stilettos.

"Here you go," he said, holding the box and pushing the shoes toward me. I jerked the orthotics out of my old shoes, shoved them into the new ones, laced up and strutted around the department store. Man, these offered the support I longed for.

"So you gonna get them or what?" he said. "Hey, they look just like my grandma's sneakers."

I yanked the box out of his arms, grabbed Sandra's hand and headed to the register to pay for the footgear from another clerk. Squeak, scrunch. Squeak, scrunch.

Take that, smart ass.

CHRISTMAS KARMA AND THE TOILET PAPER TRAIL

All I know is karma's a bitch. And never cop an attitude with an usher when you're dragging toilet paper on your shoe.

Last year, my mother braved Midwest blizzards, traffic, and the airport to visit my family of four for Christmas in California. Our fun-filled week consisted of spiked eggnog, storytelling, old movies, and the mandatory trip to San Francisco.

A commercial break during "A Christmas Story" advertised *Riverdance*, the popular Irish step-dancing group. Redheaded lads and lassies clicked across the stage.

"Forget about seeing *A Christmas Carol* or *The Nutcracker*, can we see *Riverdance*?" asked my mom.

I wanted to make her visit as memorable as possible and sprung for the good seats at the Curran Theatre in San Francisco. On Christmas Eve, we bundled up in long woolen coats, lined gloves, and scarves and loaded into our van, but before long traffic ground to a snarl.

"Gosh, we're going to be late." I said to my husband.

"No worries," Mike said, glancing at the dashboard clock. "We have an hour to park the car and find our seats. Relax."

We zoomed into the parking garage and hustled across the street to the theater, fifteen minutes to spare. Crowds clogged the lobby like stuffed animals on the shelf at Target. We shouldered our way to the ticket collector at the sold-out event.

"Tickets please," said the tall, dark-haired gentleman.

"I'm so excited," I said, holding out my ticket.

"Ten minutes till curtain time," he droned with a sigh. "Better grab your seat, lady."

We raced to the mezzanine level on the second floor. "I'll meet you inside," I said to my hubby. "Going to use the restroom." He gave me my ticket, grabbed the kids' hands and entered, my mother racing to keep up.

A sign pointed downward for "Mademoiselle." "You've got to be kidding," I mumbled to myself. The bathroom, located down two flights of stairs in a dreary sub-basement, had a line that coiled around the staircase like a serpent.

"Excuse me," I asked a buxom gal with dangly earrings. "Is this for the ladies' room?"

"Yep, only three stalls," she said with a shake of her head.

Gotta go. Too late to turn back.

The five-minute bell tolled and concerned faces stared back at me. *Oh crap*, I thought, *I'll never make it now.*

The line unexpectedly opened up. I dashed in and out, then scooted past the panicky crowd to the second floor.

Outside the mezzanine entrance, I spotted the usher, a pie-faced older woman with limp, mousey hair and beady eyes. Wearing tight khaki pants, a navy blazer, and low-heeled pumps, she cut off my entrance with her meaty arm.

"Sorry, doors closed," she said with a sneer, holding a flashlight. "You'll have to wait for a break before you can enter."

"Oh, you don't understand," I whined. "It wasn't my fault. The bathroom line was too long."

"Rules are rules. You. Must. Wait."

I peered past her shoulder pads and caught a flash of tartan and black tap shoes.

"Try and stop me," I warned and pushed her aside with my forearm like an NFL linebacker. Her flashlight clattered down the hallway. The darkness absorbed me as I groped my way to Row B.

"You almost missed the beginning," said my guy as I plopped down on my seat. He grabbed my clammy hand. "Are you OK?"

"I'm fine," I said.

Fine if you consider assault and battery no big deal.

After two and half hours of rapid-fire footwork from mini-skirted girls and leather-panted boys, the crowd stood on their feet for the final bravo.

We squeezed out the exit and I spotted a vacant handicapped restroom on the main level. I knew I shouldn't have ordered a large double cappuccino at intermission. The drive home was over an hour. Hubby took one look at my face and said, "No way. We're in a hurry. Want to beat the crowd."

Despite his protests, I lurched inside the tiny bathroom. I finished as fast as an Irish jig, swished my hands under the water, yanked down a paper towel, and rushed out the doorway. Standing a few feet from the bathroom exit was Pie Face. With her flash light. She glared at me and then her mouth curled into a smirk.

What's so funny, Shoulder Pads?

She aimed the heavy duty LED Maglite at my shoes and then my face. Through the light, I could barely make out my family leaning against the wall. My daughter was doubled over in laughter. "Oh. My. God," she said. "Look down."

Stuck to the bottom of my shoe was a five-foot toilet paper trail, double ply. My family watched in horror and delight as I bent to yank it off. I brushed my skirt smooth and felt the slight crinkle of tissue paper. "For God's sake. Let me help you," said my mother. She reached around my body to pluck off a toilet seat cover from the back of my skirt.

I pulled my coat over my head and bolted into the crowd toward the exit doors.

"Come back soon," said Pie-Face with a wide grin.

ACKNOWLEGEMENTS

My sincere thanks to the many special individuals who made this book happen, especially my extraordinary husband, Mike, who supported my writing endeavors, offered noteworthy ideas and who shares my sense of humor, and my teenage kids, Ashley and Brock, who graciously allowed me to share their development in a public forum. Please accept my apologies for any embarrassment I added to the already turbulent teenage years.

Joan Lowrey, my mother is the original Queen of Laughter, voted Best Sense of Humor, 1963. Thanks for reading to me as a child and opening our house to my teenage friends. You showed me that it's OK to relax, laugh and do your best. Charles Lowrey, my father, has always been my number one fan, teaching me the importance of hard work, persistence and risk taking.

Pastor Gerald Kovac, my moral compass, spiritual advisor and good friend, who reminds me that it is necessary to share good works with everyone

Camille Thompson, my dear friend and fellow humorist, who always drops everything to offer her sound advice and honest critiques. Penny Warner, award-winning writer, who took the time to read my first short story and encouraged me to submit to the Tri-Valley Herald. Julaina Kleist-Corwin, mentor, dreamer and writer, who shared her invaluable writing advice with me.

Patricia Marshall, talented editor, who discovered that I will avoid making decisions when possible and gently guided me during the publishing process.

Dahlynn McKowen, CEO and Publisher of Publishing Syndicate, LLC, thanks for not giving up on me when I had signed away my rights to another publication. Because of your help, I have reached my goal to be published in nearly every book in the *Not Your Mother's Book* series.

To the Tri-Valley Writers group, thanks for your advice, encouragement and support. To Hector Timourian, a gentleman and outstanding writer, and the rest of my original Tri-Valley Writers critique group, thanks for persuading me that my work was good and needed to be published.

Thank you friends and family, especially Jackie McPherran, Sharon Wernig, Karen Moore, who allowed me to make public their stories, sometimes embarrassing, sometimes awkward but always hilarious. Thanks to Mary Ney and Eugenia Murphy for believing in me and sharing my stories with others through social media.

ABOUT THE AUTHOR

Stacey Gustafson is an author, humor columnist, and blogger, experienced in the horrors of being trapped inside a pair of SPANX. Her short stories have appeared in *Chicken Soup for the Soul* and seven books in the *Not Your Mother's Book* series. Her work appears in *Midlife Boulevard, Erma Bombeck Writers' Workshop, ZestNow, More.com, Pleasanton Patch, Lost in Suburbia, Better After 50* and on her daughter's bulletin board.

Stacey's popular humor blog, *Are You Kidding Me?* is based on her suburban family and everyday life. She writes about parenting and her daily frustrations with its attendant hazards: laundry, self-checkout lanes, public restrooms, Brussels sprouts, and roundabouts.

She lives in Pleasanton, California with her husband and two teenagers, who provide an endless supply of inspiration.

Visit Stacey at StaceyGustafson.com or follow her on Twitter @RUKiddingStacey.